MICROWAVE

·LITE·

ONE-DISH MEALS
Under 350 Calories

MICROWAVE

·LITE·

ONE-DISH MEALS
Under 350 Calories

By the Editors of MICROWAVE TIMES

CB
CONTEMPORARY
BOOKS
CHICAGO

Library of Congress Cataloging-in-Publication Data

Sadlack, Janet L.
　Microwave lite one-dish meals.

　　1. Low-calorie diet—Recipes.　　2. Microwave cookery.
I. Microwave times.　　II. Title.
RM222.2.S225　　1987　　　641.5'635　　　87-13518
ISBN 0-8092-4531-0

Published by Contemporary Books, Inc.
180 North Michigan Avenue, Chicago, Illinois 60601
Manufactured in the United States of America
Library of Congress Catalog Card Number: 87-13518
International Standard Book Number: 0-8092-4531-0

Published simultaneously in Canada by Beaverbooks, Ltd.
195 Allstate Parkway, Valleywood Business Park
Markham, Ontario L3R 4T8 Canada

CONTENTS

PREFACE

Welcome to our third book in this series on lite microwave cooking. It has been exciting to see the interest in the first two books, *Microwave Cooking Lite* and *Microwave Lite Menu Cookbook*. We feel we are able to help you in two ways with these books: first, to use your microwave oven to better advantage; and second, to cook more healthy, nutritious meals.

One-dish meals is a fun concept for the microwave oven because it gives us a chance to show off what the microwave does best. A few of the dishes resemble the familiar casseroles that we often associate with one-dish meals, but many represent interesting combinations of food that are possible only from the microwave oven.

Our business, Recipes Unlimited, Inc., focuses on microwave cooking and the best way to help consumers use their microwave ovens. In 1975, we started publishing our bi-monthly publication, *The Microwave Times*. Our subscriber base has grown over the years so that we now reach thousands of oven owners and offer them a wide variety of recipes, background information, helpful hints, answers to questions, and help in adapting favorite conventional recipes to microwave preparation.

Our test kitchen and office are located in Burnsville, Minnesota, a suburb of Minneapolis. Here we test and develop recipes using a variety of ovens to help assure you success at home. We feel good recipes are important if you are really going to use your oven for more than simply reheating. We not only take special care in developing each recipe, but also test it by having another person prepare the recipe to be sure it performs the way we desire.

The staff involved in developing and testing the materials for this book include Nancy J. Johnson, Diane A. Berg, Mary Memelink, and Nancy L. Gunderson. They played a vital role in the many ideas and suggestions on the pages that follow. We can all attest to the fact that "lite" cooking *in excess* is hard on the waistline as we tasted each recipe in this book several times.

Whether your needs are for a special diet or you simply have an interest in more healthful eating, we know you will find many scrumptious one-dish meals in this book. Not only are the dishes good for you, but they show off some of the many things you and your microwave oven can accomplish with very little effort.

—Janet L. Sadlack

INTRODUCTION

One-dish dinners are more than just casseroles. Often we associate one-dish meals with starchy, heavy foods that are laden with calories, somewhat unattractive in appearance, and often mushy in texture. This certainly is not the case with the variety of recipes included in this book.

The emphasis here is on lite eating and good nutrition. Plenty of vegetables are mixed with lean cuts of meat, fish, or poultry as well as a grain or starch type of food in the form of pasta, rice, potatoes, or a bread product. Since the microwave cooks foods without scorching or drying, these combinations come out looking very attractive and have all the flavor and texture of individually cooked foods, yet offer the ease of preparation and serving of a one-dish meal.

In planning the combinations to include in this book, we looked for a variety of types of foods. We used combinations that would complement the color, flavor, and texture of the main component. Some of the ideas lent themselves well to being mixed together in true casserole form; others were best assembled on a common plate.

Eating lite is a total concept for healthy eating and living. The foods we consume as well as the quantities eaten are important. It is not just a single recipe or meal combination, but the total daily consumption over a period of time that will have a lasting effect on our well-being. This book is organized by serving occasions, so you can easily put together the type of diet you want each day. Overindulging, even with a "lite" meal, still means too many calories.

You will find a wide variety of recipes in this book. There are lite versions of many of your favorite foods as well as new recipes and ideas. Often the combinations have one or two familiar components, but take on a new look when combined with other foods. Many times the flavors will be familiar enough to be acceptable to your family, yet the end dish will help demonstrate your creativity.

One of the advantages of one-dish dinners is that there are minimal dishes to clean up. Many of the recipes can be prepared up to an hour in advance and then heated just before serving. Just remember that the longer the food has been standing and cooling, the longer it will take to reheat to serving temperature. However, preparing ahead like this really simplifies clean-up since most of the dishes can be done and forgotten before the meal is even served.

Prior to the invention of the microwave oven, one-dish meals were usually prepared in a conventional oven. Cooking in a conventional oven necessitated a good deal of time as well as the energy needed to operate the oven. The microwave oven minimizes both of

2 MICROWAVE LITE ONE-DISH MEALS

these. It is true that additional food in the microwave means additional time, but usually combinations require less time than when each food is heated in its own individual dish.

Occasionally one-dish meals were possible from a saucepan or skillet, but scorching could have been a problem. With the moist cooking of the microwave, continual stirring is not necessary and scorching is not a problem since the source of heat evenly surrounds the food rather than coming from a hot surface unit under the cooking container.

In this book, we have not totally eliminated some of the less nutritious ingredients such as fat, salt, sugar, etc., but used only the quantities necessary to enhance the natural flavor of the food being prepared. Further reductions can usually be made without affecting the end results. Salt substitutes are certainly an option when sodium is a concern. There are lower-calorie versions of many ingredients and they can often be substituted to help you meet special diet requirements. If you require a special diet, a doctor or dietitian should be consulted.

Healthy eating means monitoring your entire day's food consumption. Whether you eat three regular meals or four to five smaller meals each day, it is important to have a balance of protein, vegetables, fruit, grains, and milk products. When limiting calories, it is even more important to be sure that a balance of each of these food types is included each day.

Exercise is also a key to our well-being, but it does not replace the need to eat well. We gain weight when we consume more calories than our bodies can use. Caloric intake and physical activity need to be coordinated to help us maintain the best possible physical condition. As we age, our caloric needs decrease, which means we need to lower our food intake and/or increase our level of physical activity to prevent having to gradually buy a new wardrobe.

The recipes in this book will constitute the main part of most meals. The calories have been kept to under 400 per serving. You can add accompaniments to bring the total calories to the quantity you desire. Some of the frequently added accompaniments are listed below, along with the approximate number of calories for a serving of each:

Breads
    1 hard roll, 100
    2 bread sticks, 40
    3 crackers, 45
    1 slice whole-wheat toast, 60

Salads
    Tossed salad with lite dressing, 40
    1 carrot, 30
    1 rib celery, 7
    1 apple, 65
    1 orange, 60
    1 banana, 100

Desserts
    ½ cup fruit sherbet, 110
    ½ cup canned fruit, 60
    ½ cup frozen yogurt, 115
    ½ cup fruit-flavored yogurt, 130
    ½ cup gelatin, 80
    ½ cup pudding, 170
    1 graham cracker square, 30

Beverages
    1 glass skim milk, 90
    1 glass orange juice, 100
    1 glass apple juice, 105

When figuring caloric requirements, it is important to keep in mind the calories your body requires to function as well as the total calorie intake. To maintain weight, intake must be about the same over a period of time. To lose weight, more calories must be used than consumed. Attempt to keep the calorie range within what the body requires while at the same time eating a balance of the various foods mentioned earlier. The USDA recommends 14 to 26 calories per day for each pound of weight; depending on the level of activity. If you weigh 120 pounds, daily calorie needs are probably between 1,700 and 3,000; if you weigh 160 pounds, daily calorie needs are in the range of 2,300 to 4,000. If your lifestyle includes three meals a day with little snacking, you can divide the number of calories among the three meals. However, if you eat one main meal and several mini-meals you will need to divide up the calories a little differently.

We have planned the chapters in this book so you can find recipes for whichever lifestyle fits your individual needs. There are many family-type dishes in Chapter 3 ("Family Dishes") and Chapter 7 ("Quick and Easy"). If your family is small, you will want to check the recipes in Chapter 4 ("Dishes for One or Two"). Chapter 2 ("Dishes for Brunch and Lunch") has smaller-size meal ideas for those mini-meal needs. And, when you want something just a little extra special, turn to Chapter 5 ("Special Occasion Dishes"). Many convenience foods can be turned into appetizing lite dining. You will find a variety of suggestions and ideas in Chapter 8 ("Convenience Foods for Easy One-Dish Meals").

With these ideas at hand, maintaining good eating habits and a healthful diet should be quite easy. You are sure to be pleasantly surprised at how well you can eat and how much better you will feel. And, you will have that added peace of mind knowing that you are doing something good for yourself.

1
MICROWAVE COOKING TIPS

To help you make the best use of the recipes in this book, we encourage you to read through this short section of suggestions and explanations. The information will make the recipes more understandable as well as expand your own knowledge of microwave cooking.

TYPES OF OVENS AND POWER LEVELS

The recipes in this book were all developed and tested in 600- to 700-watt countertop microwave ovens. Many types of ovens are available today, particularly compact ovens, which have lower wattage. These lower-wattage ovens may require slightly more time than specified in the recipes in this book. A time range is given with each recipe. Start with the minimum time and add time as needed. Lower-wattage ovens will probably require the maximum time or even a little additional time to reach the degree of doneness described.

Since this book is based on combining several foods in one dish, the quantity of food is sometimes larger than normal. In most standard microwave ovens, the quantity of food and cooking dishes will always fit. However, with the smaller compact ovens, there may need to be some adjustment in dish shapes. For very small ovens, the smaller quantity recipes will be better than those yielding a larger number of servings.

Most of the recipes are cooked on the high- or full-power setting. Even foods that may be normally cooked with a lower power often need full power since in the end, cooking is slower when foods are combined. For example, when cooking meatballs, all the microwaves are being absorbed by the meatballs. However, if the recipe includes meatballs, potatoes and a green vegetable, each food receives only about one-third of the total microwave energy.

Lower-power settings are required by a few recipes. With lower-power settings, the microwave energy is pulsed on and off to achieve slower cooking. When an oven is set at 30% power, the microwave energy is on 30% of the time and the microwaves do not operate the remaining 70%. The fan remains on during the entire time, but you can often hear as the microwave energy comes on and goes off during the cooking cycle. Usually it is on a few seconds, then off a few seconds, for the total time set. When a high setting may be used, these timings are included in the recipe tips. These directions often include some standing time to slow the cooking and allow the heat to reach the center without overcooking the edges. Additional stirring and rotating are often necessary when using full-power setting.

COOKWARE

Many glass and plastic pieces are designed specifically for microwave cooking. They do not interfere with the microwave energy reaching the food and are able to withstand the heat generated by the food. For some heating, paper items are satisfactory. Glass cookware that is not specifically marked for microwave-oven use can be checked to see if it is absorbing too much microwave energy. Place the piece of cookware and a cup of water in a separate container in the oven. Microwave on high for 40 to 45 seconds. Check the warmth of the empty glass dish. If it is still fairly cool, it should work well in the microwave. If it feels warm, it will absorb too much of the microwave energy itself and cause the food to cook too slowly.

A few of the recipes call for a microwave browning dish to help brown the meat. These dishes have a special coating that becomes hot when exposed to microwave energy. After preheating the empty dish, the surface becomes very hot so that food placed on the dish begins to brown. The food cools the dish, however, so maximum browning is seen on the first side. Even when the dish is returned to the microwave with the food on it, the majority of the microwaves go to the food, so very little if any additional browning takes place from the dish. If you do not have one of these dishes, you can use a pyroceramic baking dish that is placed over a surface unit on your range. Heat the dish, add the meat, and brown it as directed. After browning, add the other ingredients, then place it in the microwave oven to complete the cooking.

ONE-DISH CONTAINERS

You will have many dishes already on your kitchen shelves that can be used for the recipes in this book. Since the food will usually go to the table in the same cooking dish, it is important to have an attractive container as well as one that will allow the microwave energy to reach the food and can withstand the heat of the food. Many serving dishes that come with dinnerware or stoneware sets are useable as long as there is no metal trim and the material does not absorb the microwave energy. If a recipe requires some browning on a surface unit, use a pyroceramic dish so that the same container can be used for the browning and then the microwave cooking.

Some of the foods that are combined will work very well on a serving dish, a serving plate, platter, or glass pizza-type plate. Just be sure the shape will fit inside the microwave oven. Again, avoid pieces with metal trim or those that will absorb microwave energy. For the smaller-size recipes, a dinner plate or individual au gratin dish is very nice. Even some of the less expensive, limited-use plastic cookware can work well for these recipes.

COVERINGS

Various coverings are used in the recipes to help hold in the heat and assure that the center of the food heats quickly. Casserole lids and plastic wrap form tight covers for foods that are steamed or simmered. Generally, they can be used interchangeably. If using the heavier plastic wraps that cling tightly, be sure to vent the dish by turning back one corner, leaving an opening of about ¼ inch. Be careful when using the thinner plastic wraps. These wraps have a lower melting point than the heavier wraps and can melt from the heat of foods like meats, and others with a high fat content.

Waxed paper is a loose-fitting covering and is often used when it is desirable to have some of the steam retained and some escape. The covering may fly off the food from the fan action in some ovens. If you use a large enough piece to tuck under the edges of the dish, it will normally stay in place. Otherwise, just weight it with a dish towel or hot pad, being careful there is no magnet.

Napkins and paper towels allow much of the moisture to evaporate, yet hold much of the heat. They are often preferred for heating bread items and crumb-topped foods as well as for preventing foods like bacon from spattering.

ROTATING, STIRRING, AND TURNING

The recipes include reminders for rotating or turning when this step may be helpful. This is more important in some ovens than in others and more critical with some foods than with others. Of course, if your oven has a turntable, rotating will not be necessary, but you may want to change the position of the dish on the turntable to help achieve more even heating.

Stirring reminders are more important since they help prevent lumping of sauces and help facilitate even cooking by exchanging the faster-cooking edges with the slower-cooking center.

To make rotating, stirring, or turning easier, you can set the time on some ovens in several intervals with a reminder that will beep when it is time to stir or rotate the food. Otherwise, you may find it helpful just to set the time in shorter intervals so cooking will cease when it is time for the stirring or rotating. These times give you an opportunity to check the progress of the food as well as assure an evenly cooked product. If you forget the rotating step, it may take a few extra minutes to get all of the food heated to the desired temperature or doneness.

SERVING TEMPERATURE

The final step of many of the recipes involves allowing time to get any partially heated items back to serving temperature. You can judge when this is done in several ways. Feeling the bottom of the dish often indicates if the contents are hot. Or, check the warmth of the food in the center of the dish. If you wish to use the oven probe, insert it in the more dense item and plan to heat to about 140°-150°F. Always reinsert the probe at least once to assure that the entire dish has reached the desired temperature, since sometimes food around the probe heats more quickly than the rest of the food.

SEQUENTIAL COOKING

An advantage of one-dish meals is that several parts can be cooked and then assembled into a final dish. For the quickest preparation, the microwave oven needs to be kept in use as much as possible. Look ahead to the next steps and do whatever chopping or mixing you can while the food is cooking. Start with foods that take less preparation since you can then begin to microwave cook more quickly.

In a few recipes, we have suggested having two dishes in the oven at the same time. Most ovens will have space for both to sit side by side. However, if your oven space does not allow for this, you can stack the dishes or use a microwave oven cooking rack. Be sure to reverse the dishes about halfway through the cooking time since the top one will normally heat more quickly than the bottom one.

CHAPTER
2
DISHES FOR BRUNCH AND LUNCH

The recipes in this chapter are perfect for those brunch and lunch occasions when you want something other than a simple soup or sandwich. One-dish egg and meat dishes, main dish salads, and quick sandwich ideas are included here.

The meals are versatile and could be enjoyed for a light supper. Some salads could double as meal accompaniments by omitting the meat. Many of the sandwiches make good mid-day or late-evening snacks. Leftover portions of most of the recipes are good to munch when hunger strikes between meals. Many of the recipes use leftover cooked meat, making preparation quick and easy.

When planning meals from this section, be sure to strive for a good nutritional balance. Most of the recipes include protein, vegetable or fruit, and starch. Adding fresh fruit or juice assures an adequate supply of vitamin C. For heartier appetites, include an additional starch such as muffins, toast, or English muffins.

Brunches and lunches can be as fun to serve as they are nutritious. Start with some recipes from this section, add your own personal touches to the meals, and share with friends.

CHICKEN–WILD RICE CHOWDER

**About 4 servings
270 calories each**

This chunky chowder makes good use of leftover cooked wild rice and chicken.

2 slices bacon

½ cup finely chopped celery

1 cup finely chopped carrots (about 2 medium)

½ cup cooked wild rice

½ cup cubed cooked chicken

¼ cup all-purpose flour

2 teaspoons instant chicken bouillon

½ teaspoon garlic salt

⅛ teaspoon sage

Dash pepper

4 cups skim milk

1 tablespoon dry sherry (optional)

1. Place bacon in 2-quart microwave-safe casserole. Cover with paper towel.

2. MICROWAVE (high) 2–3 minutes or until crisp. Set aside bacon. Reserve 1 tablespoon drippings; discard remainder. Add celery and carrots to reserved drippings.

3. MICROWAVE (high), uncovered, 4–5 minutes or until vegetables are partially cooked. Stir in rice, chicken, flour, bouillon, garlic salt, sage, and pepper. Gradually add milk, stirring until smooth. Cover.

4. MICROWAVE (high) 10–12 minutes or until mixture boils and thickens slightly, stirring twice. Stir in sherry. Crumble bacon and add to chowder.

TIPS

• For a heartier soup, increase the quantity of wild rice and chicken.

• Cooked turkey or turkey-ham can be substituted for chicken.

• Cooked white or brown rice can be substituted for wild rice.

• Individual servings can be frozen. To reheat, microwave (high) 5–6 minutes, stirring once.

CHICKEN-NOODLE SOUP

**About 5 servings,
215 calories each**

This simple-to-fix chicken soup has all the goodness of homemade soup, without the effort. Team it with crusty rolls and fruit for a nutritious lunch.

4 cups hot water

1 pound skinned chicken drumsticks (about 6)

1 small onion, chopped

1 cup thinly sliced celery

2 teaspoons instant chicken bouillon

1 teaspoon salt

⅛ teaspoon poultry seasoning

1 cup uncooked noodles (about 2 ounces)

2 cups frozen vegetable combination (broccoli, cauliflower, and carrots)

1. Combine water, chicken, onion, celery, bouillon, salt, and poultry seasoning in 2-quart microwave-safe casserole. Cover with casserole lid.

2. MICROWAVE (high) 20–25 minutes or until chicken is tender. Remove chicken and set aside to cool. Add noodles and vegetables to broth. Cover.

3. MICROWAVE (high) 10–12 minutes or until noodles are tender. Cut chicken into pieces and add to soup.

TIPS

- Leftover cooked chicken can be substituted. Use about 2 cups cubed and add to water in step 1. Reduce time in step 2 to 12–15 minutes.

- Other favorite fresh or frozen vegetables can be added in step 2.

QUICK VEGETABLE SOUP

**About 4 servings,
125 calories each**

Bacon, mixed vegetables, and tomatoes make up this tasty soup. A sprinkling of Parmesan cheese enhances the flavors.

2 slices bacon

1 16-ounce can mixed vegetables, undrained

1 16-ounce can tomatoes, undrained

½ tablespoon instant minced onion

1 teaspoon instant beef bouillon

⅛ teaspoon garlic powder

2 tablespoons grated Parmesan cheese

1. Place bacon in single layer in 1½-quart microwave-safe casserole. Cover with paper towel.

2. MICROWAVE (high) 2–3 minutes or until crisp. Set aside bacon. Reserve 1 tablespoon drippings; discard remainder. Add vegetables, tomatoes (cut into small pieces), onion, bouillon, and garlic powder to drippings. Cover with casserole lid.

3. MICROWAVE (high) 9–11 minutes or until steaming hot and flavors are blended. Crumble bacon and add to soup. Sprinkle cheese over individual bowls of soup.

TIPS

- Leftover cooked vegetables or thawed frozen vegetables can be substituted for mixed vegetables.

- If on a low-cholesterol diet, omit bacon and drippings; add 2 tablespoons imitation bacon pieces with vegetables.

TURKEY DIVANWICHES

**About 4 servings,
250 calories each**

Turkey, broccoli, and cheese blend nicely for a topping for buns or a filler for baked potatoes.

1 10-ounce package frozen chopped broccoli

1 tablespoon margarine

1 tablespoon flour

½ teaspoon salt

¼ teaspoon dry mustard

5–6 drops hot pepper sauce

½ cup skim milk

½ cup (2 ounces) shredded cheddar cheese

2 tablespoons mayonnaise or salad dressing

2 rye hamburger buns, split and toasted

4 ounces cooked turkey, thinly sliced

4 tomato slices

1. MICROWAVE (high) broccoli in package (remove foil overwrap if necessary) 5–6 minutes or until hot. Drain and set aside.

2. MICROWAVE (high) margarine in uncovered 2-cup microwave-safe measure 30–40 seconds or until melted. Stir in flour, salt, mustard, and pepper sauce until smooth. Gradually add milk, stirring until smooth.

3. MICROWAVE (high), uncovered, 1½–2 minutes or until mixture boils and thickens, stirring once. Add half of the cheese; stir until melted. Stir in mayonnaise and broccoli. Place buns cut side up on microwave-safe plate. Top each half with ¼ of the turkey, a tomato slice, and ½ cup of the broccoli mixture. Sprinkle each with about 1 tablespoon of remaining cheese.

4. MICROWAVE (high), uncovered, 2–3 minutes or until cheese is melted.

TIPS

- Four medium-size cooked potatoes can be split open and topped with filling mixture.

- Split and toasted English muffins or toasted bread slices can be substituted for hamburger buns.

DELI MELTS

Sliced meats and cheese from the deli make tasty luncheon fare when combined with fresh vegetables and served in sandwich form.

2 tablespoons margarine

½ 0.7-ounce envelope Italian salad dressing mix (2 teaspoons)

1 8-ounce loaf French bread

4 ounces cooked turkey, thinly sliced

2 ounces Swiss cheese, thinly sliced

4 ounces cooked ham, thinly sliced

6 thin slices Bermuda onion

1 small green pepper, cut into 6 slices

1 medium tomato, cut into 6 slices

½ cup alfalfa sprouts

1. MICROWAVE (high) margarine in uncovered microwave-safe dish 30–40 seconds or until melted. Stir in dressing mix. Slice French bread horizontally to make 2 pieces. Brush margarine mixture on cut sides of bread.

2. Place halves cut side up on paper plate. Top halves with layers of turkey, cheese, ham, onion, green pepper, and tomato.

3. MICROWAVE (high), uncovered, 3–4 minutes or until cheese is melted. Top with sprouts just before serving. Cut into serving pieces.

TIP

● Some small French bread loaves are 8 ounces. Otherwise, cut a section from a large loaf.

MEXICAN EGG POCKETS

**About 4 servings,
205 calories each**

Eggs scrambled with bacon, tomato, and alfalfa sprouts take on a Mexican flair when topped with cheese and taco sauce. It's a perfect filling for pocket bread.

2 slices bacon

2 tablespoons chopped green pepper

1 tablespoon water

4 eggs

¼ teaspoon salt

⅛ teaspoon tarragon leaves

Dash pepper

2 pocket-bread rounds (6-inch size)

1 cup alfalfa sprouts

1 cup chopped tomato

2 tablespoons taco sauce

¼ cup shredded cheddar cheese

1. Arrange bacon between paper toweling in 1-quart microwave-safe casserole.

2. MICROWAVE (high) 2–3 minutes or until crisp. Remove from casserole and set aside. Wipe out casserole with paper towel. Add green pepper and water to casserole and cover with casserole lid.

3. MICROWAVE (high) 1–1½ minutes or until partially cooked. Add eggs, salt, tarragon, and pepper. Mix with fork until scrambled. Cover.

4. MICROWAVE (medium-high—70%) 3–4 minutes or until eggs are just about set, stirring once. Cut pocket-bread rounds in half to form pockets. Open pockets and spoon about ⅓ cup egg mixture into each. Top with crumbled bacon, sprouts, tomato, taco sauce, and cheese.

TIPS

● The egg and vegetable mixture can also be served on 2 slices of toasted whole-wheat bread. For this combination, the calories will be about 285 each.

● To use full power instead of medium-high power in step 4, microwave 2½–3 minutes, stirring 2 or 3 times.

TOMATO-CHEESE POCKETS

**About 4 servings,
170 calories each**

A mixture of fresh vegetables, cheese, and yogurt makes the filling for these tasty pocket-bread sandwiches.

2 green onions, sliced (including tops)

1 clove garlic, minced

1½ cups (6 ounces) sliced fresh mushrooms

¼ cup chopped green pepper

1 tablespoon margarine

½ teaspoon oregano leaves

⅛ teaspoon salt

⅛ teaspoon thyme leaves

1½ cups alfalfa sprouts

1 cup chopped cucumber

½ cup (2 ounces) shredded Monterey Jack cheese

⅓ cup plain yogurt

2 whole-wheat pocket-bread rounds (6-inch size)

1 small tomato, sliced

1. Combine onions, garlic, mushrooms, green pepper, and margarine in 2-cup microwave-safe measure.

2. MICROWAVE (high), uncovered, 2–3 minutes or until tender, stirring once. Mix in remaining ingredients except pocket-bread rounds and tomato.

3. Cut pocket-bread rounds in half to form pockets. Open pockets; add tomato slices. Spoon about ⅓ cup vegetable mixture into each. Arrange on microwave-safe serving plate.

4. MICROWAVE (high), uncovered, 1½–2 minutes or until cheese begins to melt.

TIP

• When heating just 1 sandwich, reduce time in step 4 to 30–40 seconds.

VEGETARIAN ENCHILADAS

**About 4 servings,
300 calories each**

Tofu makes the creamy filling for these meatless enchiladas.

1 16-ounce can vacuum-packed
  Mexican-style corn,
  undrained

1 8-ounce can tomato sauce

1 teaspoon instant chicken
  bouillon

¼ teaspoon salt

⅛ teaspoon garlic powder

1 10½-ounce package tofu,
  undrained

2 tablespoons diced mild green
  chilies

8 corn tortillas (about 6-inch
  size)

½ cup (2 ounces) shredded
  Monterey Jack cheese

¼ cup sliced ripe olives

1. Combine corn, tomato sauce, bouillon, salt, and garlic powder in 4-cup microwave-safe measure.

2. MICROWAVE (high), uncovered, 3–4 minutes or until hot. Set aside. Place tofu and chilies in food processor or blender. Process at medium speed until smooth.

3. Moisten both sides of tortillas with water. Spread about 2 rounded tablespoons tofu mixture on each tortilla. Top each with about ¼ cup corn mixture. Roll up and place seam side down in 12- by 8-inch microwave-safe baking dish. Cover with plastic wrap.

4. MICROWAVE (high) 3–4 minutes or until heated through. Sprinkle with cheese and olives.

5. MICROWAVE (high), uncovered, 1½–2 minutes or until cheese is melted.

VEGGIES IN THE RYE

**About 6 sandwiches,
130 calories each**

Rye buns make the perfect base for these luncheon sandwiches. For more texture, toast the buns before adding the topping.

2 green onions, sliced

1 clove garlic, minced

1 cup (4 ounces) sliced fresh mushrooms

¼ cup chopped celery

1 cup shredded zucchini

¼ cup shredded carrots

½ teaspoon seasoned salt

½ cup (2 ounces) shredded Co-Jack cheese

3 rye party buns

2 tablespoons mayonnaise or salad dressing

1. Combine onions, garlic, mushrooms, and celery in 4-cup microwave-safe measure. Cover with plastic wrap.

2. MICROWAVE (high) 2–3 minutes or until vegetables are tender-crisp, stirring once. Add zucchini, carrots, salt, and cheese; mix lightly. Split buns; spread cut sides with mayonnaise; place cut side up on paper plate or paper-towel lined microwave-safe plate. Spoon vegetable mixture evenly onto buns, spreading to edges.

3. MICROWAVE (high), uncovered, 1½–2 minutes or until cheese is melted, rotating plate once.

TIP

• Other favorite cheeses can be substituted.

CONFETTI CHICKEN SALAD

**About 5 servings,
305 calories each**

Chicken and rice team with crunchy vegetables in this colorful luncheon salad. For special occasions, fill tomato flowers with the mixture.

⅔ **cup uncooked long-grain rice**

1⅓ **cups water**

½ **teaspoon salt**

8 **ounces skinned and boned chicken breast**

1 **9-ounce package frozen artichoke hearts**

¼ **cup cooking oil**

1½ **tablespoons sugar**

3 **tablespoons cider vinegar**

½ **teaspoon garlic salt**

¼ **teaspoon celery seed**

⅛ **teaspoon dry mustard**

⅛ **teaspoon pepper**

2 **green onions, sliced (including tops)**

1 **cup chopped cucumber**

⅓ **cup chopped green pepper**

1 **small tomato, cut into wedges**

1. Combine rice, water, and salt in 1½-quart microwave-safe casserole. Cover with casserole lid.

2. MICROWAVE (high) 4–5 minutes or until mixture boils. Cut chicken into bite-size pieces. Add chicken and artichoke hearts to rice. Cover.

3. MICROWAVE (high) 5–6 minutes or until mixture boils again. Then, MICROWAVE (low— 30%) 12–14 minutes or until rice is tender and chicken is done, stirring once. Uncover and cool.

4. Combine oil, sugar, vinegar, garlic salt, celery seed, mustard, and pepper in ½-pint jar. Cover and shake well to mix. Refrigerate.

5. When rice is cool, add onions, cucumber, and green pepper. Add dressing; toss lightly. Garnish with tomato wedges.

TIPS

- Rice mixture and dressing can be prepared and combined ahead. Add raw vegetables just before serving.

- To use full power instead of low power in step 3, use intervals of 3 minutes microwave and 5 minutes stand for the 12–14 minutes.

AVOCADO-CHICKEN SALAD

**About 4 servings,
350 calories each**

Fruit, avocado, and crisp vegetables combine in this uniquely flavored chicken salad.

*1 pound skinned and boned
    chicken breast*

½ teaspoon salt

1 8-ounce can pineapple chunks

1 teaspoon cornstarch

*1 11-ounce can mandarin
    oranges, drained*

2 cups torn fresh spinach

*1 medium avocado, peeled and
    cubed*

1 cup chopped cucumber

½ cup sliced celery

½ cup plain yogurt

¼ teaspoon cinnamon

1 tablespoon sliced almonds

1. Place chicken in 1-quart microwave-safe casserole. Cover with casserole lid.

2. MICROWAVE (medium-high—70%) 7–9 minutes or until no longer pink. Sprinkle with salt; set aside to cool. Refrigerate.

3. Drain juice from pineapple into 1 cup microwave-safe measure. Stir in cornstarch.

4. MICROWAVE (high), uncovered, 1–1½ minutes or until mixture boils and thickens, stirring once. Set aside to cool.

5. Cut chicken into pieces. Combine with pineapple chunks, mandarin oranges, spinach, avocado, cucumber, and celery in large salad bowl. Stir yogurt and cinnamon into cooled pineapple juice mixture. Add to salad and toss to coat. Sprinkle with sliced almonds.

TIPS

- If using leftover cooked chicken or turkey, allow about 1½ cups for this recipe.

- To use full power instead of medium-high power in step 2, microwave 4 minutes, let stand 3 minutes, rotate dish, and microwave 2–3 minutes.

SHRIMP AND VEGGIE TOSS

**About 4 servings,
215 calories each**

This refreshing salad features pasta, fresh vegetables, and shrimp.

**4 ounces uncooked rotini
(about 1¼ cups)**

1½ cups sliced fresh cauliflower

1½ cups fresh broccoli pieces

**3 green onions, sliced
(including tops)**

**6 ounces frozen cooked
shrimp, thawed**

1½ cups torn fresh spinach

1 medium tomato, chopped

½ cup chopped cucumber

½ cup plain yogurt

**1 tablespoon mayonnaise or
salad dressing**

1 tablespoon lemon juice

**1 tablespoon ranch-style salad
dressing mix**

1. Cook rotini as directed on package. Drain, rinse, and set aside.

2. Combine cauliflower, broccoli, and onions in 1½-quart microwave-safe casserole. Cover with casserole lid.

3. MICROWAVE (high) 3–4 minutes or until tender-crisp. Drain and cool. Add rotini, shrimp, spinach, tomato, and cucumber. Cover and refrigerate until chilled. Mix together yogurt, mayonnaise, lemon juice, and dressing mix. Add to salad; toss lightly.

TIPS

- Cubed cooked chicken or turkey can be substituted for shrimp. Or, use crabmeat or chopped imitation seafood.

- Other favorite macaroni-type pastas can be substituted for rotini.

TUNA-PASTA SALAD

About 5 servings, 275 calories each

Start this salad early in the day in order for flavors to be at their best.

⅓ cup apple juice

3 tablespoons white wine vinegar

3 tablespoons cooking oil

1 clove garlic, minced

1 teaspoon basil leaves

½ teaspoon salt

5 drops hot pepper sauce

4 ounces uncooked macaroni (about 1 cup)

2 cups sliced fresh cauliflower

1 cup sliced carrots (about 2 medium)

2 tablespoons water

¼ cup sliced ripe olives

1 6½-ounce can water-packed tuna, drained

4 ounces feta cheese, crumbled

1. Combine apple juice, vinegar, oil, garlic, basil, salt, and pepper sauce in jar; cover and shake well. Refrigerate.

2. Cook macaroni as directed on package. Drain, rinse, and set aside.

3. Combine cauliflower, carrots, and water in 1½-quart microwave-safe serving bowl. Cover with plastic wrap.

4. MICROWAVE (high) 3–4 minutes or until tender-crisp. Drain and cool slightly. Add olives, tuna, cheese, macaroni, and dressing mixture. Mix lightly. Refrigerate at least 3 hours to allow flavors to blend.

CHILLED SALMON CUPS

**About 4 servings,
250 calories each**

Salmon lovers will enjoy these pretty salads. Served with a crusty roll, it makes a lite lunch.

- **1 cup frozen cut asparagus**
- **½ cup water**
- **1 envelope unflavored gelatin**
- **1½ tablespoons lemon juice**
- **¼ teaspoon dill weed**
- **½ cup plain yogurt**
- **½ teaspoon prepared horseradish**
- **¼ teaspoon salt**
- **1 16-ounce can red salmon, drained**
- **4 cups torn lettuce**
- **⅓ cup chopped cucumber**
- **2 tablespoons plain yogurt**
- **¼ teaspoon dill weed**
- **Lemon wedges (optional)**

1. Place asparagus in 2-cup microwave-safe measure. Cover with plastic wrap.

2. MICROWAVE (high) 3–4 minutes or until hot. Uncover and set aside. Combine water and gelatin in 1-cup glass measure. Let stand a few minutes to soften.

3. MICROWAVE (high), uncovered, 1–1½ minutes or until dissolved. Stir in lemon juice and ⅛ teaspoon dill weed.

4. Divide asparagus among four 6-ounce custard cups or individual molds. Add 1 tablespoon gelatin mixture to each cup. To remaining gelatin mixture, add ½ cup yogurt, horseradish, and salt; mix well. Remove skin and large bones from salmon. Flake apart and mix into gelatin. Spoon mixture over asparagus; press lightly to flatten evenly. Cover and refrigerate until set, about 2 hours.

5. Divide lettuce among four serving plates. Unmold gelatin salads onto lettuce. Combine cucumber, 2 tablespoons yogurt, and ⅛ teaspoon dill weed; mix well. Spoon onto salads. If desired, garnish with lemon wedges.

CAESAR'S BEEF SALAD

**About 4 servings,
250 calories each**

Use leftover cooked beef for this upbeat salad. Serve with bread sticks and iced tea on a warm summer day.

4 cups fresh broccoli pieces

2 eggs

3 tablespoons cooking oil

3 tablespoons red wine vinegar

1 clove garlic, minced

1 teaspoon sugar

½ teaspoon salt

½ teaspoon dry mustard

5–6 drops hot pepper sauce

4 cups torn lettuce

2 cups torn fresh spinach

1 cup (4 ounces) sliced fresh mushrooms

1 cup julienne strips cooked beef (about 4 ounces)

½ cup sliced radishes

1. Place broccoli in 4-cup microwave-safe measure. Cover with plastic wrap.

2. MICROWAVE (high) 3–4 minutes or until just about tender. Drain, uncover, and cool. Place eggs in 6-ounce greased microwave-safe custard cup. Prick yolks slightly. Cover with plastic wrap.

3. MICROWAVE (high) 45–60 seconds or until edges are set. Let stand 30 seconds. Then, MICROWAVE (high) 45–60 seconds or until just about set. Uncover and cool.

4. Combine oil, vinegar, garlic, sugar, salt, mustard, and pepper sauce; mix well. Set aside.

5. Combine lettuce, spinach, mushrooms, beef, and radishes in large salad bowl. Chop eggs and add to vegetables. Add broccoli and dressing; toss lightly.

TIPS

- If desired, allow beef to marinate in the dressing mixture for about 15 minutes before adding to salad.

- Other favorite salad greens and vegetables can be substituted.

FRUITY HAM SALAD

**About 4 servings,
350 calories each**

A lite cream cheese dressing enhances the flavors of ham, fruit, and macaroni rings.

4 cups hot water

½ teaspoon salt

4 ounces uncooked macaroni
rings (about ¾ cup)

1 8-ounce can pineapple tidbits

8 ounces cubed lean ham (about
2 cups)

2 cups melon balls

1 cup red seedless grapes,
halved

½ cup thinly sliced celery

1 3-ounce package Neufchâtel
cheese

1 teaspoon Dijon-style mustard

Lettuce leaves (optional)

1. Combine water and salt in 2-quart microwave-safe mixing bowl.

2. MICROWAVE (high), uncovered, 5–6 minutes or until boiling. Add macaroni.

3. MICROWAVE (high), uncovered, 6–7 minutes or until macaroni is tender, stirring once or twice. Drain, rinse, and set aside.

4. Drain pineapple, reserving juice. Combine pineapple, ham, melon balls, grapes, and celery in 2-quart salad bowl. Set aside.

5. MICROWAVE (high) Neufchâtel cheese in uncovered microwave-safe dish 30–40 seconds or until softened. Gradually blend in reserved pineapple juice and mustard, mixing well. Pour over fruit mixture; add macaroni and toss lightly. Refrigerate at least 2 hours or until chilled. If desired, serve on lettuce leaves or in a pineapple or melon half.

TIPS

● Cubed cooked chicken or turkey can be substituted for part or all of ham.

● Other fresh fruit can be substituted for melon and grapes.

CRAB-ASPARAGUS QUICHE

**About 5 servings,
275 calories each**

Rice makes the easy and tasty crust for this colorful seafood quiche.

1 *8-ounce package frozen cut asparagus*

2 *cups hot cooked rice*

1 *cup (4 ounces) shredded Swiss cheese*

1 *egg, beaten*

1 *tablespoon margarine*

¼ *teaspoon salt*

8 *ounces frozen imitation crabmeat sticks, thawed*

2 *eggs, beaten*

2 *tablespoons skim milk*

1 *2-ounce jar diced pimiento, drained*

1 *tablespoon lemon juice*

4 *drops hot pepper sauce*

¼ *teaspoon garlic salt*

1. MICROWAVE (high) asparagus in package (remove foil overwrap if necessary) 5–6 minutes or until hot. Drain and set aside.

2. Combine rice, ½ cup of the Swiss cheese, 1 egg, margarine, and salt in mixing bowl. Mix well. Press into bottom and up sides of 9-inch microwave-safe pie plate. Set aside.

3. Cut crabmeat sticks into bite-size pieces. Combine with 2 eggs, milk, pimiento, lemon juice, pepper sauce, garlic salt, remaining ½ cup Swiss cheese, and asparagus; mix well. Pour into crust.

4. MICROWAVE (medium—50%), uncovered, 10–12 minutes or until center is set, rotating dish once. Let stand about 5 minutes before cutting into wedges to serve.

TIPS

- Thawed frozen cooked crabmeat, shrimp, or lobster can be substituted for imitation crabmeat.

- To use full power instead of medium power in step 4, microwave filling mixture in mixing bowl 2–3 minutes or until heated, stirring once. Pour into crust and microwave 2½–3½ minutes, rotating plate twice.

- Individual servings can be frozen. To reheat, microwave (medium-high—70%) 4½–5½ minutes, rotating plate once.

HAM-MUSHROOM QUICHE

**About 5 servings,
155 calories each**

Thin ham slices make the crust for this interesting quiche variation featuring spinach and mushrooms.

  1 **10-ounce package frozen chopped spinach**

  2 **cups (8 ounces) sliced fresh mushrooms**

  3 **green onions, sliced (including tops)**

  2 **eggs, beaten**

  ¾ **cup skim milk**

  ½ **cup (2 ounces) shredded Swiss cheese**

  ¼ **cup dry bread crumbs**

5–6 **drops hot pepper sauce**

  ⅛ **teaspoon nutmeg**

  5 **thin slices lean ham (about 5 ounces)**

1. MICROWAVE (high) spinach in package (remove foil wrap if necessary) 5–6 minutes or until hot. Drain, squeezing out excess moisture. Set aside. Combine mushrooms and onions in 1-quart microwave-safe casserole.

2. MICROWAVE (high), uncovered, 3–4 minutes or until tender. Add spinach, eggs, milk, cheese, bread crumbs, pepper sauce, and nutmeg; mix well.

3. Arrange ham slices in bottom and up sides of 9-inch microwave-safe pie plate. Carefully pour egg mixture into crust. Cover with plastic wrap.

4. MICROWAVE (medium—50%) 12–14 minutes or until just about set, rotating plate once. Let stand 5 minutes before cutting into wedges.

TIPS

● Chopped broccoli can be substituted for spinach.

● If desired, use turkey-ham.

● To use full power instead of medium power in step 4, heat egg mixture in casserole 2–3 minutes or until mixture starts to thicken, stirring twice. Pour into crust. Microwave 2–3 minutes, rotating plate 3 times.

● Individual servings can be frozen. To reheat, microwave (medium-high—70%) 4½–5½ minutes.

TORTILLA-SPINACH PIE

**About 5 servings,
190 calories each**

Tortillas are the easy crust for an egg and spinach filling. Add fresh fruit and crusty rolls for an interesting brunch or lunch.

1 small onion, chopped

1 cup (4 ounces) sliced fresh mushrooms

1 10-ounce package frozen chopped spinach

2 eggs, beaten

1 cup low-fat cottage cheese

½ teaspoon salt

⅛ teaspoon nutmeg

Dash pepper

½ cup (2 ounces) shredded Monterey Jack cheese

3 flour tortillas (about 7-inch size)

1. Combine onion and mushrooms in 2-quart microwave-safe casserole.

2. MICROWAVE (high), uncovered, 2–3 minutes or until just about tender. Add spinach.

3. MICROWAVE (high), uncovered, 4–5 minutes or until spinach is thawed, stirring once. Drain, squeezing excess moisture from spinach. Mix in eggs, cottage cheese, salt, nutmeg, pepper, and Jack cheese.

4. Line 9-inch microwave-safe pie plate with tortillas, allowing them to extend up sides and overlap on bottom. Pour spinach mixture into crust; spread evenly. Cover with waxed paper.

5. MICROWAVE (high) 6–7 minutes or until edges begin to set, rotating plate once. Then, MICROWAVE (medium—50%) 8–10 minutes or until center is set, rotating dish once. Let stand 5 minutes before cutting into wedges for serving.

TIPS

- Leftovers are good served cold. Or, if desired, reheat each serving by microwaving 1–1½ minutes.

- To use full power instead of medium power in step 5, use intervals of 2 minutes microwave and 2 minutes stand for the 8–10 minutes.

HEARTY POACHED EGGS

**About 4 servings,
225 calories each**

*Make your own hash from frozen hash browns. Then, gently cook an egg in the center
of each serving.*

1 12-ounce package frozen hash
browns (4 patties)

½ cup chopped celery

¼ cup chopped green pepper

1 cup finely chopped turkey
ham

½ cup skim milk

1 teaspoon instant chicken
bouillon

¼ teaspoon dill weed

Dash pepper

4 eggs

Salt and pepper

1 small tomato, chopped

¼ cup shredded cheddar cheese

1. Combine hash browns, celery, and green pepper in 8-inch round microwave-safe pie plate or baking dish. Cover with plastic wrap.

2. MICROWAVE (high) 5½–6½ minutes or until hot, stirring once. Stir in ham, milk, bouillon, dill weed, and pepper. Cover.

3. MICROWAVE (high) 3–4 minutes or until heated through. Using back of spoon, make 4 indentations in mixure; break an egg into each. Sprinkle eggs with salt and pepper. Cover.

4. MICROWAVE (medium-high—70%) 4–5 minutes or until eggs are desired doneness, rotating plate once. Sprinkle with tomato and cheese. Cover and let stand a few minutes or until cheese is melted.

TIP

● To use full power instead of medium-high power in step 4, microwave 3–4 minutes, rotating dish twice.

GARDENER'S OMELET DELIGHT

**About 4 servings,
145 calories each**

This omelet is perfect when fresh vegetables are bountiful.

1 cup fresh broccoli pieces

*1 cup chopped zucchini
(1 medium)*

*1 cup (4 ounces) sliced fresh
mushrooms*

2 tablespoons chopped onion

1 tablespoon water

4 eggs

1 teaspoon diced pimiento

¼ teaspoon salt

¼ teaspoon dry mustard

⅛ teaspoon basil leaves

Dash pepper

¼ cup shredded cheddar cheese

*1 tablespoon grated Parmesan
cheese*

1 small tomato, chopped

1. Combine broccoli, zucchini, mushrooms, onion, and water in 8- or 9-inch microwave-safe pie plate. Cover with plastic wrap.

2. MICROWAVE (high) 4–4½ minutes or until vegetables are tender, stirring once. Remove ½ cup vegetables and set aside. Beat together eggs, pimiento, salt, mustard, basil, and pepper. Pour over vegetables in pie plate. Cover with plastic wrap.

3. MICROWAVE (medium-high—70%) 3–3½ minutes or until edges are just about set. Sprinkle with reserved vegetables. Top with cheeses. Cover.

4. MICROWAVE (medium-high—70%) 1–1½ minutes or until center is just about set. Let stand 5 minutes. Top with tomato. Serve cut into wedges.

TIP

● To use full power instead of medium-high power in step 3, microwave 2½–3 minutes, rotating pie plate twice. In step 4, microwave 45–60 seconds, rotating plate once.

CHEESE AND BROCCOLI CREPES

About 12 crepes, 180 calories each

A lite mushroom sauce tops these broccoli and cheese-filled crepes. Make the crepes ahead or have some on hand in the freezer for super-fast preparation.

12 crepes

  4 cups chopped fresh broccoli

1½ cups low-fat cottage cheese

  ½ cup (2 ounces) shredded mozzarella cheese

  2 tablespoons grated Parmesan cheese

  1 egg, beaten

  1 clove garlic, minced

  1 cup (4 ounces) sliced fresh mushrooms

  1 tablespoon margarine

  1 cup chicken broth

  2 tablespoons cornstarch

  ¼ teaspoon salt

  2 tablespoons snipped fresh parsley

1. Prepare crepes using favorite crepe recipe. Set aside.

2. MICROWAVE (high) broccoli in covered 2-quart microwave-safe casserole 5–6 minutes or until just about tender. Drain. Add cheeses and egg; mix well. Place about 2 rounded tablespoons of mixture down center of each crepe. Roll up with filling inside. Place seam side down in 12- by 8-inch microwave-safe baking dish. Set aside.

3. Combine garlic, mushrooms, and margarine in 4-cup microwave-safe measure.

4. MICROWAVE (high), uncovered, 1½–2 minutes or until tender-crisp. Stir in broth, cornstarch, and salt, mixing well.

5. MICROWAVE (high), uncovered, 2½–3½ minutes or until mixture boils and thickens, stirring once. Pour over crepes. Cover with waxed paper.

6. MICROWAVE (medium-high—70%) 8–10 minutes or until heated through (150°F). Sprinkle with parsley just before serving.

TIPS

- Two packages frozen chopped broccoli can be substituted for fresh. Increase time in step 2 to 9–10 minutes.

- Flour tortillas or leftover thin pancakes can be substituted for crepes.

- To use full power instead of medium-high power in step 6, reduce time to 6–7 minutes, rotating dish twice.

- To quickly defrost frozen crepes, microwave 3–4 minutes, removing defrosted crepes each minute.

CHAPTER
3
FAMILY DISHES

With our fast-paced lifestyle, it becomes increasingly difficult to find time to share conversation or a family meal together. So, when the opportunities arise, it is important to make the most of them. One of the nice things that often happens when there is a microwave oven in the kitchen is that more family members become interested in the food preparation. This, too, can be time well spent in talking about the day's activities. The recipes in this section can provide the nucleus for some quality family time—either in preparing meals together or in eating them together.

The majority of recipes in this section are for four or five servings. If this is not your normal family size, you can easily tailor the recipe to meet your family's needs. Several of the recipes have "tips" for freezing individual servings for another meal. Refer to Chapter 5 for freezing hints. These "extras" in the freezer are perfect for families on the go who need to eat at several different times.

You will find the ingredients and preparation of these recipes quite basic, yet versatile. There are some dishes that combine the foods in true "casserole" form and other combinations where each food maintains its own identity. The recipes usually include a protein source as well as vegetable and starch. If your family prefers another type of vegetable, substitutions can be made with minimal time change as long as the form (fresh, frozen, or canned) and quantity are the same.

The recipes in this section are grouped by meat or protein type. Thus, you will find the fish recipes listed together as well as the poultry, ground beef, and meatless sections.

You and your family can be more creative microwave cooks than you ever thought possible. And, with the ideas in this section, you will be eating combinations that are healthier, too. We hope you will take the opportunity to enjoy many of these dishes with your family soon.

CHICKEN TETRAZZINI

**About 5 servings,
330 calories each**

The entire family is sure to enjoy this colorful combination of chicken, spaghetti, and vegetables. There's just a hint of caraway in this delicate blend of flavors.

6 ounces uncooked spaghetti, broken in half

1 clove garlic, minced

1 small onion, chopped

2 tablespoons water

1 pound skinned and boned chicken breast

2 cups (8 ounces) sliced fresh mushrooms

3 cups fresh broccoli pieces

¼ cup evaporated skim milk

¾ teaspoon salt

Dash pepper

⅛ teaspoon caraway seed

2 tablespoons grated Parmesan cheese

2 tablespoons diced pimiento

1. Cook spaghetti as directed on package. Drain, rinse, and set aside.

2. Combine garlic, onion, and water in 2-quart microwave-safe casserole.

3. MICROWAVE (high), uncovered, 2–3 minutes or until tender. Cut chicken into thin strips. Add to casserole along with mushrooms and broccoli; mix lightly. Cover with casserole lid.

4. MICROWAVE (high) 6–7 minutes or until chicken is just about cooked, stirring once or twice. Add remaining ingredients, including drained spaghetti; mix lightly. Cover.

5. MICROWAVE (high) 3–5 minutes or until heated through, stirring once.

TIPS

- About 2 cups cubed cooked chicken can be used in place of the chicken breast.

- Individual servings can be frozen. To reheat, add 2 tablespoons water and microwave (high) 5–6 minutes, stirring twice.

SAUCY CHICKEN AND VEGETABLES

About 4 servings, 285 calories each

Chicken and rice is always a favorite. You and your family are sure to enjoy this version, including fresh vegetables and a flavorful mushroom sauce.

½ cup uncooked long-grain rice

1 14½-ounce can chicken broth

1 tablespoon diced pimiento

2 cups fresh cauliflower pieces

2 cups fresh broccoli pieces

12 ounces skinned and boned chicken breast, cut into serving pieces

Natural chicken browning and seasoning powder

1 cup (4 ounces) sliced fresh mushrooms

1 clove garlic, minced

1 tablespoon margarine

2 tablespoons flour

½ teaspoon salt

Dash pepper

1. Combine rice, 1 cup of broth (reserve remainder), and pimiento in 10- by 6-inch microwave-safe baking dish. Cover with plastic wrap.

2. MICROWAVE (high) 5–6 minutes or until mixture boils. Then, MICROWAVE (medium— 50%) 7–8 minutes or until rice is just about tender. Stir and arrange rice evenly in dish. Place cauliflower pieces over rice at each end of dish. Place broccoli in center of dish and arrange chicken pieces between cauliflower and broccoli. Sprinkle chicken with browning powder. Cover with plastic wrap.

3. MICROWAVE (high) 8–9 minutes or until chicken is done and vegetables are tender, rotating dish once. Let stand covered.

4. Combine mushrooms, garlic, and margarine in 2-cup microwave-safe measure.

5. MICROWAVE (high), uncovered, 2–3 minutes or until partially cooked. Stir in flour, salt, pepper, and remaining chicken broth until flour is dissolved.

6. MICROWAVE (high), uncovered, 2½–3 minutes or until mixture boils and thickens, stirring once. Pour sauce over chicken and vegetables.

TIPS

● To substitute instant chicken bouillon for broth, use 1⅔ cups water and 1 teaspoon bouillon; decrease salt addition to ¼ teaspoon.

● If you do not have the browning powder, sprinkle chicken pieces with cornflake crumbs and paprika.

● To use full power for medium power in step 2, use intervals of 2 minutes microwave and 3 minutes stand for the 7–8 minutes.

CURRIED CHICKEN WITH DUMPLINGS

About 5 servings, 325 calories each

Cranberry sauce tops each of the dumplings that crown this creamed chicken dish.

2 tablespoons margarine

¼ cup unsifted all-purpose flour

2 teaspoons instant chicken bouillon

½ teaspoon curry powder

2½ cups skim milk

2 cups cubed cooked chicken or turkey

8 ounces fresh broccoli spears

1 cup buttermilk baking mix

⅓ cup skim milk

3 tablespoons cranberry sauce

1. MICROWAVE (high) margarine in uncovered 4-cup microwave-safe measure 30–45 seconds or until melted. Stir in flour, bouillon, curry powder, and milk until smooth.

2. MICROWAVE (high), uncovered, 7–8 minutes or until mixture boils and thickens, stirring 2 or 3 times. Stir in chicken. Set aside.

3. Arrange broccoli in shallow 2-quart microwave-safe baking dish with stems toward outside of dish. Cover with plastic wrap.

4. MICROWAVE (high) 3½–4½ minutes or until just about tender. Turn stems toward inside of dish. Pour chicken mixture over broccoli.

5. MICROWAVE (high), uncovered, 3–4 minutes or until boiling hot.

6. Meanwhile, combine baking mix and milk, mixing just until moistened. Spoon by tablespoonful onto hot mixture at outer edge of dish, making about 5 dumplings. Make a small indentation in each dumpling with spoon. Spoon a rounded ½ tablespoon cranberry sauce into each indentation.

7. MICROWAVE (high), uncovered, 3½–4½ minutes or until dumplings are no longer doughy.

TIPS

● The sauce has a mild curry flavor. If you really enjoy curry, increase amount to 1 teaspoon.

● A 10-ounce package frozen broccoli spears can be substituted for fresh. Microwave (high) in package 4–5 minutes or until thawed and then arrange in baking dish, top with chicken mixture and continue as directed.

CALICO CHICKEN CASSEROLE

**About 4 servings,
300 calories each**

Strips of chicken breast cook with a flavored rice mix in this easy casserole. Asparagus and pimiento add color and flavor.

3 green onions, sliced (including tops)

1 clove garlic, minced

1 tablespoon margarine

1 8-ounce package chicken-flavored rice and vermicelli mix

3 cups hot water

½ tablespoon soy sauce

8 ounces skinned and boned chicken breast

1 8-ounce package frozen cut asparagus

1 2-ounce jar sliced pimiento

1. Combine onions, garlic, and margarine in 1½-quart microwave-safe casserole.
2. MICROWAVE (high), uncovered, 1½–2 minutes or until tender. Add rice mixture (not seasoning packet).
3. MICROWAVE (high), uncovered, 2–3 minutes or until vermicelli starts to brown. Add seasoning packet, hot water, and soy sauce; mix lightly. Cut chicken into strips; add to rice. Cover with casserole lid.
4. MICROWAVE (high) 4–5 minutes or until mixture boils. Then, MICROWAVE (low—30%) 12–14 minutes or until rice and chicken are just about tender. Add asparagus and pimiento. Cover.
5. MICROWAVE (high) 4–5 minutes or until asparagus is tender. Let stand covered 5 minutes; fluff with fork.

TIPS

- Frozen peas can be substituted for asparagus.

- Individual servings can be frozen. To reheat, add 2 tablespoons water and microwave (high) 5–6 minutes, stirring once.

- To use full power instead of low power in step 4, use intervals of 2 minutes microwave and 3 minutes stand for the 12–14 minutes.

SWEET 'N' SOUR CHICKEN

**About 5 servings,
200 calories each**

This Chinese combination of chicken chunks, tender-crisp vegetables, and a tasty sauce includes pasta rather than the traditional rice. We think you will enjoy the change of pace.

2 ounces uncooked linguine, broken into 2-inch lengths

1 cup sliced carrot

1 tablespoon water

8 ounces skinned and boned chicken breast

2 green onions, sliced (including tops)

1 clove garlic, minced

1 cup sliced zucchini (about 1 medium)

½ cup sliced green pepper

1 8-ounce can pineapple chunks in fruit juice

Water

2 tablespoons packed brown sugar

1 tablespoon cornstarch

1 tablespoon soy sauce

1 teaspoon grated fresh ginger root

1 tablespoon sliced pimiento

1. Cook linguine as directed on package. Drain, rinse, and set aside. Combine carrots and 1 tablespoon water in 1½-quart microwave-safe casserole. Cover with casserole lid.

2. MICROWAVE (high) 2½–3 minutes or until just about tender. Cut chicken into 1-inch pieces. Add to carrots; mix lightly. Add onions, garlic, zucchini, and green pepper.

3. MICROWAVE (high), uncovered, 5–6 minutes or until chicken is tender and vegetables are tender-crisp, stirring once. Set aside.

4. Drain juice from pineapple into 2-cup microwave-safe measure. Add water to make 1 cup. Blend in brown sugar, cornstarch, soy sauce, and ginger until smooth.

5. MICROWAVE (high), uncovered, 2½–3½ minutes or until mixture boils and thickens, stirring once. Pour over chicken mixture. Add pineapple chunks, pimiento, and linguine; mix lightly. Cover.

6. MICROWAVE (high) 3–4 minutes or until heated through, stirring once.

TIP

● To substitute ground ginger for ginger root, use ¼ teaspoon.

CHICKEN TARRAGON PLATTER

**About 4 servings,
345 calories each**

A tarragon marinade enhances the flavor of chicken in this attractive dish. Cheese-coated potato wedges and tomato pieces complete the entree.

3 tablespoons tarragon vinegar

1½ tablespoons cooking oil

1½ tablespoons water

2 cloves garlic, minced

2 green onions, sliced

1 teaspoon salt

½ teaspoon tarragon leaves

1 frying chicken, quartered (about 3 pounds)

1 large potato, peeled (about 8 ounces)

1 tablespoon margarine

2 tablespoons grated Parmesan cheese

¼ teaspoon onion salt

⅛ teaspoon paprika

1 tomato, cut into 8 wedges

1. Combine vinegar, oil, water, garlic, onions, salt, and tarragon in measuring cup. Remove skin from chicken. Place chicken in large plastic bag. Pour vinegar mixture over chicken; turn bag to coat evenly. Secure bag and refrigerate at least 4 hours, rearranging once to coat chicken.

2. Remove chicken from marinade; pat lightly with paper towels to dry. Arrange chicken toward edge of 12-inch microwave-safe serving plate. Cover with waxed paper.

3. MICROWAVE (high) 10 minutes or until chicken begins to cook, rotating plate once. Drain and set aside covered. Cut potato in half lengthwise; then cut each half into 4 wedges.

4. MICROWAVE (high) margarine in uncovered shallow dish or plate 45–60 seconds or until melted. Combine Parmesan cheese, onion salt, and paprika on waxed paper. Coat potato wedges with margarine; dip each in cheese mixture to coat. Arrange on serving plate between chicken quarters. Cover with plastic wrap.

5. MICROWAVE (high) 13–18 minutes or until chicken is done, rotating plate once or twice. Add tomato wedges.

6. MICROWAVE (high), uncovered, 1–2 minutes or until tomatoes are heated through. Brush chicken with additional marinade if desired.

TIPS

● If desired, substitute 3 pounds of favorite chicken pieces for quartered chicken.

● If microwave oven does not accommodate a 12-inch round serving plate, use an oval or oblong plate that will fit inside oven.

STUFFED TURKEY TENDERLOINS

**About 4 servings,
320 calories each**

Broccoli and cheese-filled turkey tenderloins are cooked atop a vegetable-bread stuffing in this tasty dish.

1 10-ounce package frozen
  chopped broccoli

¼ teaspoon oregano leaves

½ cup (2 ounces) shredded
  cheddar cheese

1 pound turkey tenderloins
  (about 2)

Salt

1 cup (4 ounces) sliced fresh
  mushrooms

3 green onions, sliced
  (including tops)

1 tablespoon margarine

1½ cups (3 ounces) dry herb-
  seasoned stuffing mix

½ cup water

1 tablespoon dry bread crumbs

1 tablespoon grated Parmesan
  cheese

¼ teaspoon paprika

1. MICROWAVE (high) broccoli in package (remove foil overwrap if necessary) 5–6 minutes or until tender, turning package over once. Drain. Combine with oregano and cheese in mixing bowl; mix lightly. Set aside.

2. Place turkey tenderloins between plastic wrap. Pound with flat side of meat mallet or rolling pin until ¼ inch thick. Sprinkle with salt. Cut each in half to make 4 pieces. Top each with ¼ cup broccoli mixture (reserve remainder). Roll up with filling inside, starting at narrow end. Set aside.

3. Combine mushrooms, onions, and margarine in 10- by 6-inch microwave-safe baking dish.

4. MICROWAVE (high), uncovered, 2–3 minutes or until tender. Stir in stuffing mix and water. Add reserved broccoli mixture; mix lightly.

5. Combine bread crumbs, Parmesan cheese, and paprika on waxed paper. Coat each turkey roll with crumbs. Place rolls on stuffing mixture. Cover with plastic wrap.

6. MICROWAVE (medium—50%) 14–16 minutes or until turkey is done, rotating dish once.

TIPS

● To use full power instead of medium power in step 6, reduce time to 6–8 minutes, rotating dish 3 times.

● Individual servings can be frozen. To reheat, microwave (medium-high—70%) 8–10 minutes, rotating dish once.

TURKEY ORIENTAL

**About 5 servings,
305 calories each**

This combination of turkey strips, vegetables, and cashews is perfect over rice.

⅔ **cup uncooked long-grain rice**

1 **pound turkey tenderloins (about 2)**

2 **green onions, sliced (including tops)**

1 **8-ounce package frozen cut asparagus**

1 **cup fresh cauliflower pieces**

1 **cup (4 ounces) sliced fresh mushrooms**

1 **clove garlic, minced**

¼ **cup water**

1 **tablespoon cornstarch**

2 **tablespoons dry sherry (optional)**

½ **teaspoon salt**

2–3 **drops hot pepper sauce**

1 **tablespoon sliced pimiento**

3 **tablespoons cashews**

1. Cook rice as directed on package while preparing turkey mixture.

2. Cut turkey into thin bite-size strips. Combine turkey, onions, asparagus, cauliflower, mushrooms, and garlic in 2-quart microwave-safe casserole. Cover with casserole lid.

3. MICROWAVE (high) 10–12 minutes or until turkey is done, stirring twice. Combine water and cornstarch until smooth. Stir into turkey mixture. Add sherry, salt, pepper sauce, and pimiento; mix well.

4. MICROWAVE (high), uncovered, 2½–3 minutes or until mixture boils and thickens slightly, stirring once. Sprinkle with cashews and serve over rice.

TIPS

- If desired, substitute 1 pound skinned and boned chicken breast for turkey.

- About 2 cups fresh asparagus can be substituted for frozen.

- Individual servings can be frozen. To reheat, add 2 tablespoons water and microwave (high) 5–6 minutes.

SPANISH EGGPLANT CASSEROLE

**About 6 servings,
255 calories each**

Eggplant slices cook atop a Spanish rice mixture. What a flavorful way to utilize the often abundant eggplant crop.

1 pound ground turkey

1 medium onion, chopped

½ cup chopped green pepper

1 cup quick-cooking rice

1 16-ounce can tomatoes, undrained

1 8-ounce can tomato sauce

1 teaspoon oregano leaves

½ teaspoon chili powder

1 small eggplant, cut into 1-inch slices

½ cup (2 ounces) shredded cheddar cheese

¼ cup grated Parmesan cheese

Paprika

1. Crumble turkey into 12- by 8-inch microwave-safe baking dish. Add onion and green pepper.

2. MICROWAVE (high), uncovered, 5–6 minutes or until no longer pink, stirring once. Stir in rice, tomatoes (cut tomatoes into small pieces), tomato sauce, oregano, and chili powder. Cover with plastic wrap.

3. MICROWAVE (high) 5–6 minutes or until hot and bubbly, stirring once. Arrange eggplant slices on top. Cover with plastic wrap.

4. MICROWAVE (high) 9–11 minutes or until eggplant is tender, rotating dish once. Top with cheeses; sprinkle with paprika.

5. MICROWAVE (high), uncovered, 2–3 minutes or until cheeses are melted.

TIP

● Extra-lean ground beef can be substituted for turkey.

TURKEY-RICE PATTIES WITH CHEESY CAULIFLOWER

**About 6 servings,
240 calories each**

Rice and chopped apple add to the flavor of these moist turkey patties. Cauliflower makes a nice addition for a complete meal-in-one dish.

1 medium onion, chopped

1 tablespoon margarine

1 pound ground turkey

2 medium apples, chopped

1¼ cups quick-cooking rice

1 tablespoon parsley flakes

*½ to 1 teaspoon poultry
seasoning*

½ teaspoon salt

Dash pepper

1 egg, slightly beaten

*1 teaspoon natural meat
browning and seasoning
powder*

*1 medium green pepper, seeded
and cut into 6 rings*

4 cups fresh cauliflower pieces

*¼ cup pasteurized process
cheese spread (Cheez Whiz)*

1. Combine onion and margarine in 2-quart microwave-safe mixing bowl.

2. MICROWAVE (high), uncovered, 2–2½ minutes or until onion is tender. Mix in turkey, apples, rice, parsley, poultry seasoning, salt, pepper, and egg. Divide into six portions. Shape each into a patty about 4 inches in diameter. Place on 12-inch round microwave-safe serving plate. Sprinkle with browning powder. Cover with plastic wrap.

3. MICROWAVE (high) 10–11 minutes or until just about done. Top each patty with green pepper ring. Arrange cauliflower around patties. Cover with plastic wrap.

4. MICROWAVE (high) 5–6 minutes or until cauliflower is tender. Spoon cheese spread onto cauliflower. Let stand until melted.

TIPS

● If microwave oven does not accommodate a 12-inch round plate, use an oval or oblong plate that will fit inside oven.

● Broccoli can be substituted for cauliflower.

● If browning powder is not available, brush patties with soy sauce.

● Individual servings can be frozen. To reheat, microwave (medium-high—70%) 4–5 minutes, rotating dish once.

TORTILLA PIE

**About 5 servings,
350 calories each**

*Spinach and a tasty meat sauce are layered between tortillas. Just cut into wedges to
serve.*

1 10-ounce package frozen
chopped spinach

1 pound ground turkey

1 small onion, chopped

1 clove garlic, minced

½ cup chopped green pepper

1 8-ounce can tomato sauce

2 tablespoons dry bread crumbs

¾ teaspoon chili powder

½ teaspoon salt

½ cup low-fat cottage cheese

3 flour or corn tortillas (about
7-inch size)

1 cup (4 ounces) shredded
Monterey Jack cheese

1. MICROWAVE (high) spinach in package (remove foil overwrap if necessary) 4–5 minutes or until thawed, turning package over once. Drain and set aside.

2. Crumble turkey into 1-quart microwave-safe casserole. Add onion, garlic, and green pepper.

3. MICROWAVE (high), uncovered, 5–6 minutes or until turkey is no longer pink, stirring once. Stir in tomato sauce, bread crumbs, chili powder, and salt. Mix spinach with cottage cheese.

4. Place a tortilla in the bottom of 9-inch microwave-safe pie plate. Top with a scant cup of meat mixture, spreading to edge of plate. Spread with about ⅓ of the spinach and Jack cheese. Repeat with two more layers of tortilla, meat, spinach, and cheese.

5. MICROWAVE (medium-high—70%), uncovered, 10–12 minutes or until center is hot, rotating plate once. Let stand about 5 minutes before cutting into wedges for serving.

TIPS

● Extra-lean ground beef can be substituted for turkey.

● To use full power instead of medium-high power in step 5, wait to add the last layer of cheese. Cover with waxed paper and reduce time in step 5 to 7–9 minutes, rotating plate 3 times. Sprinkle with cheese and let stand a few minutes until cheese is melted.

FISH ROLL-UPS ON RICE

**About 4 servings,
240 calories each**

Sole roll-ups are cooked on a bed of vegetable-rice pilaf.

1½ cups (6 ounces) sliced fresh
  mushrooms

 1 cup sliced zucchini (about 1
  medium)

1½ cups shredded carrots (about
  3 medium)

 3 green onions, sliced
  (including tops)

 1 tablespoon margarine

 ¾ cup water

 ½ cup uncooked long-grain rice

 1 teaspoon instant chicken
  bouillon

 1 teaspoon parsley flakes

 1 pound sole fillets

Salt

Paprika

Snipped fresh parsley (optional)

1. Combine mushrooms, zucchini, carrots, onions, and margarine in 1½-quart microwave-safe casserole.

2. MICROWAVE (high), uncovered, 4–5 minutes or until vegetables are tender-crisp. Add water, rice, bouillon, and parsley. Cover with casserole lid.

3. MICROWAVE (high) 4–5 minutes or until mixture boils. Then, MICROWAVE (low—30%) 12–14 minutes or until rice is just about tender.

4. Cut fillets into serving-size pieces. Sprinkle with salt. Roll up and place seam side down on rice mixture. Sprinkle with paprika. Cover.

5. MICROWAVE (high) 4–5 minutes or until fish flakes apart easily with fork. If desired, garnish with snipped fresh parsley.

TIPS

● Other favorite fish fillets can be substituted.

● To use full power instead of low power in step 3, use intervals of 2 minutes microwave and 3 minutes stand for the 12–14 minutes.

"SOLE FOOD" PLATTER

**About 4 servings,
215 calories each**

*Rolled fillet of sole combines with an appealing blend of vegetables for a meal that is
simple enough for family dining, yet attractive enough to enjoy with guests.*

*1 10-ounce package frozen
  broccoli spears*

*12 ounces small new potatoes
   (about 6)*

1 pound sole fillets

Salt

2 tablespoons margarine

2 tablespoons lemon juice

½ teaspoon dill weed

Paprika

*1 small tomato, cut into wedges
  (optional)*

1. Unwrap broccoli; place in center of 12-inch round microwave-safe serving plate. Scrub potatoes; cut each in half and place cut side down around broccoli. Cover with plastic wrap.

2. MICROWAVE (high) 9–11 minutes or until vegetables are tender. Lift one corner of plastic wrap and carefully drain juices. Remove plastic wrap. Alternate broccoli and potato halves around outside part of plate. Cut sole fillets into serving pieces. Sprinkle with salt.

3. MICROWAVE (high) margarine in uncovered small microwave-safe dish 30–45 seconds or until melted. Add lemon juice and dill. Brush on fillets. Roll up each and place seam side down in center of plate. Brush again with margarine mixture. Sprinkle with paprika. Cover with plastic wrap.

4. MICROWAVE (high) 4–5 minutes or until fish flakes apart easily with fork. Drizzle remaining margarine mixture over fish and vegetables. Garnish with tomato wedges.

TIPS

● If microwave oven does not accommodate a 12-inch round serving plate, use an oval or oblong platter that will fit inside oven.

● Other favorite fish fillets can be substituted.

VEGETABLE-COD PRIMAVERA

About 5 servings, 295 calories each

A medley of fresh vegetables and chunks of cod combine with fettuccini noodles in this delicious entree. Even those not fond of fish will enjoy the delicate flavors of this dish.

4 ounces uncooked fettuccini

2 slices bacon

1 medium onion, chopped

2 tablespoons flour

1 teaspoon beau monde seasoning

½ teaspoon salt

Dash white pepper

1¼ cups skim milk

2 cups fresh broccoli pieces

1 cup fresh cauliflower pieces

1 cup chopped carrots (about 2 medium)

2 tablespoons water

1 pound cod or torsk fillets, cut into 1-inch pieces

1 cup (4 ounces) sliced fresh mushrooms

2 tablespoons grated Parmesan cheese

1. Cook fettuccini as directed on package. Drain, rinse, and set aside.

2. Cut bacon into small pieces; place in 2-quart microwave-safe casserole. Add onion. Cover with paper towel.

3. MICROWAVE (high) 2–3 minutes or until bacon is crisp. Reserve 1 tablespoon drippings in casserole; discard remainder. Stir in flour, seasoning, salt, pepper, and milk until blended.

4. MICROWAVE (high), uncovered, 4–5 minutes or until mixture boils and thickens, stirring once. Set aside.

5. Combine broccoli, cauliflower, and carrots in 4-cup microwave-safe measure. Add 2 tablespoons water. Cover with plastic wrap.

6. MICROWAVE (high), uncovered, 5–6 minutes or until just about tender; drain. Add to sauce along with cod and mushrooms. Cover with casserole lid.

7. MICROWAVE (high) 4–5 minutes or until fish flakes apart easily, stirring once.

8. Arrange fettuccini on microwave-safe serving plate, spreading toward edge of plate. Spoon fish mixture into center. Sprinkle with Parmesan cheese.

9. MICROWAVE (high), uncovered, 2–3 minutes or until heated through.

TIPS

● Other vegetable combinations can be used. Use a total of about 4 cups for these timings.

● Celery seed can be substituted for Beau Monde seasoning. Reduce amount to ½ teaspoon.

SEAFOOD SUPREME

**About 5 servings,
185 calories each**

Tender-crisp vegetables add color and flavor to this dish featuring macaroni shells and seafood.

4 ounces uncooked macaroni shells (about 1 cup)

2 cups (8 ounces) sliced fresh mushrooms

2 cups fresh broccoli pieces

1 cup diagonally sliced carrots (about 2 medium)

1 clove garlic, minced

1 tablespoon margarine

Water

½ tablespoon cornstarch

1 teaspoon instant chicken bouillon

½ teaspoon lemon juice

Dash hot pepper sauce

8 ounces frozen imitation crabmeat sticks, thawed

1. Cook macaroni as directed on package. Drain, rinse, and set aside.

2. Combine mushrooms, broccoli, carrots, garlic, and margarine in 1½-quart microwave-safe casserole. Cover with casserole lid.

3. MICROWAVE (high) 8–9 minutes or until vegetables are tender-crisp, stirring once. Drain vegetables into 2-cup microwave-safe measure, draining well. Add water to make ¾ cup. Mix in cornstarch, bouillon, lemon juice, and pepper sauce until blended.

4. MICROWAVE (high), uncovered, 1–1½ minutes or until mixture boils and thickens, stirring once. Add to vegetables along with macaroni. Cut crabmeat sticks into 1-inch pieces; add to sauce. Mix lightly.

5. MICROWAVE (high), uncovered, 2–3 minutes or until heated through.

TIP

• If desired, substitute 8 ounces frozen crab or shrimp for crabmeat sticks.

DILLY SALMON BAKE

**About 4 servings,
295 calories each**

This flavorful combination of fresh new potatoes, springtime peas, and canned salmon is enhanced by the addition of dill.

**12 ounces small new potatoes
    (about 6)**

 2 tablespoons water

 2 cups fresh shelled peas

 **1 15½-ounce can pink salmon,
    drained**

 ½ cup plain yogurt

 **2 tablespoons mayonnaise or
    salad dressing**

 ½ teaspoon salt

 ½ teaspoon dill weed

 ⅛ teaspoon pepper

 **1 green onion, sliced (including
    top)**

1. Scrub potatoes; slice ⅛ inch thick. Place in 1½-quart microwave-safe casserole. Add water. Cover with casserole lid.

2. MICROWAVE (high) 6–7 minutes or until potatoes are just about tender, rearranging once. Add peas. Cover.

3. MICROWAVE (high) 4–5 minutes or until peas are hot. Drain. Remove skin and larger bones from salmon; break salmon into chunks and add to peas along with yogurt, mayonnaise, salt, dill weed, and pepper. Mix lightly. Cover.

4. MICROWAVE (high) 3–4 minutes or until heated through, stirring once. Garnish with green onion.

TIPS

- A 10-ounce package frozen peas can be substituted for fresh peas.

- Red salmon can be used, but calories will be slightly higher.

ITALIAN TUNA CASSEROLE

**About 4 servings,
260 calories each**

An Italian-flavored rice mixture is the interesting base for tuna and green beans in this family casserole.

  1 medium onion, chopped

  1 clove garlic, minced

½ tablespoon cooking oil

1¼ cups quick-cooking rice

  1 16-ounce can tomatoes, undrained

  1 8-ounce can tomato sauce

  1 6½-ounce can water-packed tuna, drained

¼ cup sliced ripe olives

¼ teaspoon oregano leaves

¼ teaspoon salt

  1 10-ounce package frozen Italian-cut green beans

½ cup (2 ounces) shredded mozzarella cheese

  1 tablespoon grated Parmesan cheese

1. Combine onion, garlic, and oil in 2-quart microwave-safe casserole.

2. MICROWAVE (high), uncovered, 2–3 minutes or until just about tender. Stir in rice, tomatoes (cut tomatoes into small pieces), tomato sauce, tuna, olives, oregano, and salt. Cover with casserole lid.

3. MICROWAVE (high) 5–6 minutes or until mixture boils. Stir rice and top with beans. Cover with casserole lid.

4. MICROWAVE (high) 7–8 minutes or until beans are tender. Sprinkle with cheeses. Cover and let stand a few minutes or until cheeses are melted.

TIP

● Other vegetables such as peas and carrots or mixed vegetables can be substituted for beans.

FAMILY BEEF ROAST WITH VEGETABLES

**About 5 servings,
325 calories each**

Traditional vegetables crown this beef roast. Since most roasts include more meat than what is needed for 5 servings, we allowed for about ⅓ of the roast to be left over and used in another meal.

2½ pounds sirloin tip beef roast

2 tablespoons dry onion soup mix

Pepper

5 medium potatoes, peeled (about 1 pound)

3 medium carrots, cut into 2-inch pieces

1 small head cabbage (about 1 pound)

4 ounces fresh mushrooms (about 1 cup)

1 rib celery, cut into 2-inch pieces

1. Trim all fat from meat. Place meat on microwave-safe roasting rack. Sprinkle with soup mix, rubbing into meat. Sprinkle with pepper. Cover with waxed paper.

2. MICROWAVE (high) 5–6 minutes or until edges are hot. Place potatoes and carrots around roast. Cover with waxed paper.

3. MICROWAVE (medium—50%) 30 minutes. Turn roast over and rearrange vegetables, spooning juices over meat and vegetables. Cut cabbage into wedges. Place around roast along with mushrooms and celery. Cover with plastic wrap.

4. MICROWAVE (medium—50%) 25–30 minutes or until internal temperature of meat is 150°F, rotating rack once. Transfer meat to serving plate. Cover with foil and let stand about 10 minutes. Spread vegetables on roasting rack and cover with plastic wrap.

5. MICROWAVE (high) 4–6 minutes or until tender. Slice about ⅔ of roast. Arrange vegetables on plate. If desired, serve with meat juices.

TIPS

- Remaining ⅓ of roast can be sliced or cubed, cooled, and frozen. Use in recipes that call for cooked meat.

- Meat can also be cooked in a cooking/roasting bag. Place bag in a microwave-safe baking dish, secure with string, and use timings as directed.

- Less tender meats such as this are best cooked with a lower power setting.

POPEYE'S STROGANOFF HOTDISH

**About 5 servings,
350 calories each**

There is no need to precook the noodles in this easy, nutritious one-dish meal.

1 pound boneless beef round
   steak

2 tablespoons flour

1 tablespoon cooking oil

1 small onion, chopped

2 cups (8 ounces) sliced fresh
   mushrooms

1 10½-ounce can condensed beef
   broth

¼ cup water

3 cups uncooked noodles (about
   4½ ounces)

¼ teaspoon salt

⅛ teaspoon pepper

1 teaspoon catsup

½ teaspoon prepared mustard

4 cups fresh spinach (about 5
   ounces), coarsely chopped

1 cup plain yogurt

1. Cut meat into thin strips. Coat with flour. Heat oil in shallow 1½-quart pyroceramic casserole over medium-high heat on range. Add meat and onion and brown on all sides. Stir in any remaining flour, mushrooms, broth, water, noodles, salt, pepper, catsup, and mustard. Cover with casserole lid.

2. MICROWAVE (high), 12–14 minutes or until noodles are tender, stirring twice. Add spinach. Cover.

3. MICROWAVE (high) 3–4 minutes or until spinach is tender. Stir in yogurt.

TIP

• An 8-ounce can sliced mushrooms, undrained, can be substituted for fresh mushrooms.

MEATBALL-CHILI COMBO

**About 5 servings,
315 calories each**

The spicy flavors of chili combine with zucchini and meatballs in this simple dish.

1 **pound lean ground beef**

3 **tablespoons dry bread crumbs**

2 **tablespoons skim milk**

¼ **teaspoon salt**

Dash pepper

1 **medium onion, chopped**

1 **clove garlic, minced**

1 **tablespoon water**

1½ **teaspoons chili powder**

½ **teaspoon salt**

¼ **teaspoon basil leaves**

¼ **teaspoon oregano leaves**

1 **14½-ounce can tomatoes, undrained**

1 **15½-ounce can red kidney beans, undrained**

4 **cups sliced zucchini (about 4 medium)**

½ **cup chopped green pepper**

1. Combine ground beef, bread crumbs, milk, ¼ teaspoon salt, and pepper; mix well. Shape into 1-inch meatballs. Place on microwave-safe meat rack. Cover with waxed paper.

2. MICROWAVE (high) 6–7 minutes or until no longer pink, rotating dish once. Set aside. Combine onion, garlic, and water in shallow 2-quart microwave-safe casserole. Cover with casserole lid.

3. MICROWAVE (high) 2–3 minutes or until just about tender. Add remaining ingredients (cut tomatoes into small pieces). Add meatballs and mix lightly. Cover.

4. MICROWAVE (high) 14–16 minutes or until zucchini is tender and mixture is hot, stirring twice.

TIP

● Individual servings can be frozen. To reheat, microwave (high) 5–6 minutes, stirring twice.

MUSHROOM-HAMBURGER PLATTER

About 4 servings, 345 calories each

Mushroom-filled patties, broccoli pieces, and potato wedges cook together in this easy and attractive dinner.

1 cup (4 ounces) sliced fresh mushrooms

3 green onions, sliced (including tops)

2 baking potatoes (about 12 ounces)

2 tablespoons dry bread crumbs

1 tablespoon grated Parmesan cheese

¼ teaspoon paprika

1 tablespoon margarine

1 pound lean ground beef

¼ cup dry bread crumbs

½ teaspoon salt

⅛ teaspoon pepper

1 tablespoon chili sauce or catsup

2 cups fresh broccoli pieces

1. Combine mushrooms and onions in 2-cup microwave-safe measure.

2. MICROWAVE (high), uncovered, 2–2½ minutes or until tender. Drain and set aside.

3. Scrub potatoes; cut each into 6 wedges. Combine 2 tablespoons bread crumbs, Parmesan cheese, and paprika on waxed paper.

4. MICROWAVE (high) margarine in small uncovered microwave-safe dish 30–45 seconds or until melted. Brush cut sides of potato wedges with margarine. Coat wedges with crumbs. Arrange on outer edge of 12-inch round microwave-safe serving plate. Cover with plastic wrap.

5. MICROWAVE (high) 3–4 minutes or until potatoes are hot. While potatoes are cooking, combine ground beef, ¼ cup bread crumbs, salt, and pepper; mix well. Divide into eight portions. Roll each into ball and then flatten on waxed paper to 3-inch circle. Divide mushroom mixture evenly among four of the patties. Top each with a plain patty; pinch edges to seal. Arrange patties in center of plate with potatoes. Top with chili sauce. Make clusters of potato wedges and arrange broccoli between clusters. If necessary, place any remaining broccoli in center of plate. Drizzle vegetables with any remaining margarine. Cover with plastic wrap.

6. MICROWAVE (high) 9–11 minutes or until meat is done and vegetables are tender. If necessary, drain juices before serving.

TIPS

● If microwave oven does not accommodate a 12-inch round plate, use an oval or oblong shape that will fit inside of oven.

● Patties can also be prepared without the mushroom filling.

CRESCENT SUPPER CASSEROLE

About 5 servings, 330 calories each

Crescent roll triangles top this popular ground beef and vegetable casserole.

- **1 pound lean ground beef**
- **2 cups (8 ounces) sliced fresh mushrooms**
- **1 16-ounce package frozen Japanese-style vegetables**
- **1 10¾-ounce can condensed tomato soup**
- **2½ tablespoons dry onion soup mix (½ envelope)**
- **1 4-ounce tube refrigerated crescent roll dough**
- **1 tablespoon cornflake crumbs**

Paprika

1. Crumble ground beef into 1½-quart microwave-safe casserole. Add mushrooms.
2. MICROWAVE (high), uncovered, 6–7 minutes or until meat is no longer pink, stirring once. Drain. Stir in frozen vegetables and soups. Cover with casserole lid.
3. MICROWAVE (high) 9–10 minutes or until mixture is boiling hot, stirring once. Unwrap crescent roll dough. Cut each section into 3 triangles. Place on casserole. Sprinkle with cornflake crumbs and paprika.
4. MICROWAVE (medium—50%), uncovered, 6–8 minutes or until topping is no longer doughy, rotating dish once. Let stand 5 minutes before serving.

TIPS

- Other frozen vegetables can be substituted.

- To use full power instead of medium power in step 4, use intervals of 2 minutes microwave and 2 minutes stand for the 6–8 minutes total time.

HOT NACHO PLATTER

**About 5 servings,
325 calories each**

This colorful, tasty "South of the Border" fare is as delicious as it is appealing.

½ *pound lean ground beef*

1 *small onion, chopped*

1 *15-ounce can kidney beans, undrained*

1 *8-ounce can tomato sauce*

2 *tablespoons taco seasoning mix (½ of a 1¼-ounce envelope)*

2 *cups shredded lettuce*

1 *small tomato, chopped*

1½ *cups slightly crushed corn chips (3 ounces)*

½ *cup (2 ounces) shredded cheddar cheese*

1. Crumble ground beef into 1-quart microwave-safe casserole. Add onion.

2. MICROWAVE (high), uncovered, 3–4 minutes or until meat is no longer pink. Drain; stir to break meat into small pieces. Add beans, tomato sauce, and seasoning mix; mix well. Cover with casserole lid.

3. MICROWAVE (medium—50%) 8–10 minutes or until flavors are blended and mixture is thickened. Arrange lettuce around outer edge of microwave-safe serving plate. Top with tomato. Spoon hot meat mixture into center. Top with chips and cheese.

TIPS

● To use full power instead of medium power in step 3, reduce time to 6–8 minutes, stirring twice. Allow mixture to stand 5 minutes before using.

● Assembled mixture does not reheat well. If fewer servings are needed, assemble and heat smaller quantities. Then, refrigerate any leftover meat mixture. When ready to use, reheat the meat before assembling with other ingredients.

CORNED BEEF AND CABBAGE CASEROLE

**About 5 servings,
230 calories each**

This quick and easy family dish includes many of your favorite sandwich flavors.

6 cups shredded cabbage
(about 1 small head)

3 medium carrots, shredded
(about 1½ cups)

¼ cup chopped green pepper

8 ounces thinly sliced deli-
style corned beef, cut into
strips

2 tablespoons water

½ cup plain yogurt

½ cup (2 ounces) shredded
Swiss cheese

⅔ cup crushed crisp rye
crackers (about 2 ounces)

¼–½ teaspoon caraway seed

1. Combine cabbage, carrots, green pepper, corned beef, and water in 2-quart microwave-safe casserole. Cover with casserole lid.

2. MICROWAVE (high) 10–11 minutes or until cabbage is tender-crisp, stirring once. Stir in yogurt, cheese, crackers, and caraway; mix well. Cover.

3. MICROWAVE (high) 3–4 minutes or until heated through.

TIP

• Other forms of corned beef can be used, but the calories are higher than in the type you purchase in a deli.

AUTUMN PORK DINNER

**About 6 servings,
240 calories each**

Tender pork rolls are arranged on a platter with acorn squash rings and broccoli in this pretty harvest-time dinner.

½ cup water

6 dried prunes

1 medium acorn squash (about 1½ pounds)

1¼ pounds pork tenderloin, cut into 6 pieces

Salt

1 medium apple, sliced

1½ tablespoons flour

1 tablespoon margarine

3 tablespoons dry sherry

½ teaspoon salt

½ teaspoon summer savory

2 tablespoons currant jelly

3 cups fresh broccoli pieces

1. Combine water and prunes in 1-cup microwave-safe measure.

2. MICROWAVE (high), uncovered, 1–1½ minutes or until hot. Set aside.

3. Prick squash with fork several times. Place on paper towel in microwave oven.

4. MICROWAVE (high) 7–9 minutes or until just about tender, turning squash over once. Set aside.

5. Place pieces of pork between plastic wrap. Pound with flat side of meat mallet or rolling pin to ¼-inch thickness. Sprinkle with salt. Remove prunes from liquid (reserve liquid) and cut each in half. Place 2 halves on each pork piece. Divide apple slices among pork. Roll up pork with fruit inside. Fasten with toothpicks. Coat rolls with flour.

6. Heat margarine in frying pan over medium-high heat on range. Add rolls and brown on all sides. While meat is browning, cut squash crosswise into 6 slices. Remove seeds and arrange near edge of 12-inch round microwave-safe serving plate. Place a pork roll on each squash slice. Add any remaining flour, liquid from prunes, sherry, salt, savory, and jelly to drippings in pan; bring to boil. Pour over rolls. Place broccoli in center of plate. Cover with plastic wrap.

7. MICROWAVE (high) 8–10 minutes or until broccoli is tender, rotating plate once. Let stand about 5 minutes before serving.

TIPS

● Frozen broccoli spears can be substituted for fresh.

● If microwave oven does not accommodate a round plate, use an oval or oblong shape that will fit inside of oven.

PORK CHOPS WITH VEGGIE BUNDLES

About 4 servings, 330 calories each

Sliced potatoes make the base while bundles of vegetables provide the topping for this pork chop dish. A mild, wine-flavored sauce adds that special finishing touch.

1 tablespoon cooking oil

4 loin pork chops (about 1 pound)

3 medium potatoes, sliced

½ teaspoon instant chicken bouillon

¼ cup water

2 medium carrots

1 rib celery

2 green onions

¼ cup dry white wine

1 tablespoon snipped fresh parsley

Salt and pepper

1. Heat oil in shallow 2-quart pyroceramic casserole over medium-high heat on range. Add chops and brown on both sides. Remove chops and discard drippings. Add potatoes, bouillon, and water to casserole. Cover with casserole lid.

2. MICROWAVE (high) 2–3 minutes or until potatoes are hot. Top with chops. Cut carrots and celery into matchstick pieces, about 2 inches long. Divide into four bundles. Cut green onions in half lengthwise. Wrap an onion piece around each vegetable bundle. Place on chops. Drizzle with wine. Cover.

3. MICROWAVE (medium—50%) 17–19 minutes or until chops are tender, rotating dish once or twice and basting with sauce. Sprinkle with parsley, salt, and pepper.

TIPS

• Chicken broth can be substituted for wine.

• To use full power instead of medium power in step 3, use intervals of 4 minutes microwave and 4 minutes stand for the 17–19 minutes.

PORK AND CABBAGE TERIYAKI

**About 4 servings,
340 calories each**

Tender strips of pork combine with Chinese cabbage, mushrooms, and tomato in this tasty stir-fry meal.

1 pound boneless lean pork

1 medium onion, chopped

¼ cup teriyaki sauce

1 tablespoon cornstarch

⅔ cup uncooked long-grain rice

1⅓ cups water

¼ teaspoon salt

4 cups thinly sliced Chinese cabbage (Napa)

1 cup (4 ounces) sliced fresh mushrooms

1 tablespoon diced pimiento

1 tablespoon margarine

1 tomato, cut into wedges

1. Cut pork into thin slices. Combine with onion, sauce, and cornstarch in 2-quart microwave-safe casserole. Mix lightly and set aside while cooking rice.

2. Combine rice, water, and salt in 1-quart microwave-safe casserole. Cover with casserole lid.

3. MICROWAVE (high) 4–5 minutes or until mixture boils. Then, MICROWAVE (low—30%) 10–12 minutes or until rice is just about tender. Let stand covered. Stir pork mixture. Cover with casserole lid.

4. MICROWAVE (high) 4–5 minutes or until pork is no longer pink, stirring once. Add cabbage, mushrooms, pimiento, and margarine; mix lightly. Cover.

5. MICROWAVE (high) 3–4 minutes or until vegetables are tender-crisp, stirring once. Add tomato and mix lightly. Spoon rice onto microwave-safe serving plate. Top with pork mixture.

6. MICROWAVE (high), uncovered, 1–2 minutes or until heated through.

TIPS

● If you have leftover cooked rice, use about 2 cups and increase time in step 6 to 3–4 minutes.

● To use full power instead of low power in step 3, use intervals of 2 minutes microwave and 3 minutes stand for the 10–12 minutes.

COUNTRY PORK

**About 5 servings,
345 calories each**

*Cubes of pork simmer in a tasty sauce that includes apples, carrots, and brussels sprouts.
Then, it is all served on a bed of noodles.*

1 pound cubed lean pork

1 tablespoon flour

1 tablespoon margarine

1 medium onion, sliced

1 clove garlic, minced

2 medium apples, peeled and
    sliced

3 medium carrots, cut into
    1-inch pieces (2 cups)

¼ cup dry white wine

½ cup water

¾ teaspoon salt

⅛ teaspoon ground sage or
    poultry seasoning

Dash pepper

2½ cups uncooked noodles
    (3½ ounces)

1 10-ounce package frozen
    brussels sprouts

½ teaspoon marjoram leaves

1. Coat pork with flour. Heat margarine in shallow 2-quart pyroceramic casserole over medium-high heat on range. Add pork and onion and brown on all sides, stirring occasionally. Add garlic, apples, carrots, wine, water, salt, sage, and pepper; mix lightly. Cover with casserole lid.

2. MICROWAVE (high) 15–17 minutes or until carrots are tender, stirring twice. Meanwhile, cook noodles as directed on package. Drain, rinse, and set aside. Add brussels sprouts and marjoram to pork; mix lightly. Cover.

3. MICROWAVE (high) 5–6 minutes or until sprouts are tender, stirring once. Arrange noodles on microwave-safe serving plate, spreading toward edge of plate. Spoon pork mixture into center.

4. MICROWAVE (high), uncovered, 2–3 minutes or until heated through.

TIPS

● If wine is omitted, increase water to ¾ cup.

● Individual servings can be frozen. To reheat, add 1 tablespoon water and microwave (medium-high—70%) 9–11 minutes, stirring once.

PORK FAJITAS

**About 8 servings,
210 calories each**

This meal in a tortilla is fun to serve for many occasions. Make the guacamole while the pork is marinating.

12 ounces boneless lean pork,
½ inch thick

1 lime

1 clove garlic, minced

½ teaspoon cumin

¼ teaspoon salt

¼ teaspoon chili powder

1 avocado, peeled and pitted

⅓ cup low-fat cottage cheese

1 clove garlic

1 teaspoon lemon juice

3–4 drops hot pepper sauce

½ tablespoon cornstarch

1 medium onion, sliced thin

1 green pepper, seeded and
sliced thin

1 small tomato, cut into
wedges

8 flour tortillas (about 7-inch
size)

Picante sauce (optional)

1. Cut pork into thin strips; place in 1½-quart microwave-safe casserole. Squeeze lime and pour juice over pork. Add minced garlic, cumin, salt, and chili powder; mix to coat pork evenly. Let stand about 30 minutes to marinate.

2. Meanwhile, make guacamole by combining avocado, cottage cheese, whole garlic, lemon juice, and pepper sauce in food processor or blender container. Process on medium speed until smooth. Set aside.

3. Cover meat with casserole lid. MICROWAVE (high) 5–6 minutes or until no longer pink, stirring once. Stir in cornstarch. Add onion, green pepper, and tomato; mix lightly.

4. MICROWAVE (high), uncovered, 3–4 minutes or until vegetables are tender and sauce boils and thickens, stirring once. Set aside. Wrap tortillas in plastic wrap.

5. MICROWAVE (high) 1–1½ minutes or until warm. Spread each tortilla with about 1 tablespoon guacamole. Top each with a scant ⅓ cup of meat mixture. Add picante sauce, if desired. Fold in 3 sides of tortilla to enclose filling.

TIPS

• For maximum juice from the lime, microwave (high) 15–20 seconds before squeezing.

• This recipe makes more guacamole than is needed. Store extra in covered container in refrigerator and use as a dip or as an accompaniment with other Mexican foods.

ORIENTAL PORK AND RICE

**About 4 servings,
255 calories each**

*Marinated pork cubes combine with rice and vegetables for a family supper dish with an
Oriental flair. Be sure to allow at least an hour for the meat to marinate.*

3 green onions, sliced
  (including tops)

1 clove garlic, minced

3 tablespoons soy sauce

1 tablespoon dry sherry

1 teaspoon brown sugar

12 ounces cubed lean pork

½ cup uncooked long-grain rice

¾ cup water

2 cups (8 ounces) sliced fresh
  mushrooms

1 cup shredded carrots (about 2
  medium)

1 6-ounce package frozen pea
  pods

1. Combine onions, garlic, soy sauce, sherry, and
   brown sugar in plastic bag; mix well. Add pork
   and turn bag to coat evenly. Let stand at least 1
   hour to marinate.

2. Combine rice, water, mushrooms, and carrots in
   2-quart microwave-safe casserole. Cover with lid.

3. MICROWAVE (high) 5–6 minutes or until
   mixture boils. Then, MICROWAVE (low—30%)
   12–14 minutes or until rice is just about tender.
   Add pork and marinade; mix lightly. Cover.

4. MICROWAVE (high) 5–6 minutes or until pork is
   just about done. Add pea pods; mix lightly.
   Cover.

5. MICROWAVE (high) 2–3 minutes or until pea
   pods are hot. Mix lightly.

TIPS

- To use full power instead of low power in step 3, use intervals of 2 minutes microwave
  and 3 minutes stand for the 12–14 minutes.

- Individual servings can be frozen. To reheat, add 1 tablespoon water and microwave
  (high) 5–6 minutes, stirring once.

GERMAN POTATO SALAD DINNER

**About 4 servings,
245 calories each**

Turkey ham and zucchini add interest to this slightly tangy version of German potato salad.

3 cups cubed potatoes (about 3 medium)

¼ cup water

½ teaspoon salt

2 cups sliced zucchini (about 2 medium)

2 slices bacon

2 tablespoons red wine vinegar

½ teaspoon cornstarch

½ teaspoon dill weed

½ teaspoon Dijon-style mustard

12 ounces turkey ham, sliced ¼-inch thick

1 medium tomato, coarsely chopped

2 tablespoons grated Parmesan cheese

1. Combine potatoes, water, and salt in 1½-quart microwave-safe casserole. Cover with casserole lid.

2. MICROWAVE (high) 7–9 minutes or until just about tender, stirring once. Add zucchini. Cover.

3. MICROWAVE (high) 3–4 minutes or until tender. Set aside. Place bacon in 2-cup microwave-safe measure. Cover with paper towel.

4. MICROWAVE (high) 1½–2½ minutes or until crisp. Remove bacon and set aside. Reserve 1 tablespoon drippings in measure; discard remainder. Drain liquid from potatoes into measure. Add vinegar, sugar, cornstarch, dill weed, and mustard; mix well.

5. MICROWAVE (high) 1–1½ minutes or until mixture boils. Pour over potato mixture; toss lightly. Push mixture to center of casserole. Tuck ham slices around sides, overlapping as necessary. Spread potato mixture evenly in dish. Top with tomato and cheese. Crumble bacon over top.

6. MICROWAVE (high), uncovered, 3–4 minutes or until warm.

TIP

● Tomato and cheese can be omitted; sprinkle top with paprika.

SUNSHINE YAM CASSEROLE

**About 4 servings,
260 calories each**

*Orange juice, cinnamon, and apples enhance the goodness of ham and yams, which are
served in a colorful ring of broccoli.*

1½ *pounds yams (about 3
   medium)*

 1 *cup orange juice*

 ½ *teaspoon cinnamon*

 ⅛ *teaspoon salt*

1½ *cups (8 ounces) cubed
   turkey-ham*

 1 *apple, cored and sliced thin*

 2 *tablespoons snipped fresh
   parsley*

10 *ounces trimmed fresh
   broccoli (about 4 cups)*

Salt (optional)

1. Prick yams with fork; place in 2-quart
   microwave-safe casserole. Cover with casserole
   lid.

2. MICROWAVE (high) 8–10 minutes or until just
   about tender, rearranging once. Remove from
   casserole and cool enough to handle. Peel, slice,
   and return to casserole. Add orange juice,
   cinnamon, salt, ham, apple, and parsley; mix
   lightly.

3. Cut broccoli into 2½-inch-long pieces with stalk
   no more than ½ inch thick. Arrange around edge
   of large 10- to 12-inch microwave-safe serving
   plate, overlapping as necessary. Spoon yam
   mixture into center. Cover with plastic wrap.

4. MICROWAVE (high) 7–8 minutes or until
   broccoli is tender and yam mixture is heated
   through.

TIPS

● A 10-ounce package frozen broccoli spears can be substituted for fresh. Microwave
  (high) 2–3 minutes or until spears can be separated. Arrange on plate and continue as
  directed.

● Sweet potatoes can be substituted for yams.

CORN CHOWDER

**About 5 servings,
230 calories each**

Bits of bacon and lots of vegetables give this soup its delicious flavor.

3 slices bacon

1 small onion, chopped

2 medium potatoes, diced (1¼ cups)

1 clove garlic, minced

¼ cup water

1 10-ounce package frozen cut corn

1 cup shredded zucchini (about 1 medium)

1 12-ounce can evaporated skim milk

1 cup water

2 tablespoons flour

2 teaspoons instant chicken bouillon

Dash pepper

1. Place bacon in 2-quart microwave-safe casserole. Cover with paper towel.

2. MICROWAVE (high) 2½–3½ minutes or until bacon is crisp. Remove bacon and set aside. Reserve 1 tablespoon drippings in casserole; discard remainder. Add onion, potatoes, garlic, and ¼ cup water to drippings. Cover with casserole lid.

3. MICROWAVE (high) 7–8 minutes or until potatoes are tender, stirring once. Add corn, zucchini, and milk; mix lightly. Combine water and flour until smooth. Stir into vegetable mixture along with bouillon, pepper, and crumbled bacon.

4. MICROWAVE (high), uncovered, 14–16 minutes or until mixture boils and thickens slightly, stirring twice.

TIP

• Chopped fresh spinach can be substituted for zucchini.

POLENTA PIE

**About 5 servings,
270 calories each**

An easy-to-make cornmeal crust is the interesting base for this flavorful Italian-style entree.

1 cup water
⅛ teaspoon salt
⅓ cup yellow cornmeal
8 ounces Italian sausage
1 small onion, chopped
1 clove garlic, minced
2 cups sliced zucchini (about 2 medium)
1 cup (4 ounces) sliced fresh mushrooms
½ teaspoon salt
½ teaspoon basil leaves
¼ teaspoon oregano leaves
1 8-ounce can tomato sauce
½ cup (2 ounces) shredded mozzarella cheese

1. MICROWAVE (high) water in uncovered 2-cup microwave-safe measure 2–3 minutes or until boiling. Stir in salt and cornmeal.

2. MICROWAVE (high), uncovered, 1–1½ minutes or until mixture boils and thickens, stirring once. Spread evenly over bottom and up sides of 8-inch round microwave-safe baking dish. Set aside. Crumble sausage into 1-quart microwave-safe casserole. Add onion and garlic.

3. MICROWAVE (high), uncovered, 4–5 minutes or until sausage is no longer pink, stirring once. Drain well; break meat into small pieces. Add zucchini, mushrooms, salt, basil, and oregano. Cover with casserole lid.

4. MICROWAVE (high) 3–4 minutes or until vegetables are tender-crisp, stirring once. Stir in tomato sauce; pour into cornmeal crust.

5. MICROWAVE (high), uncovered, 4–4½ minutes or until hot. Top with cheese.

6. MICROWAVE (high), uncovered, 1½–2 minutes or until cheese is melted.

TIP

● To further reduce the calories, use a microwave-safe collander or strainer for cooking the sausage so the fat drains away as the meat cooks.

VEAL-NOODLE BAKE

**About 5 servings,
305 calories each**

Ground veal, noodles, and vegetables are combined in this delicious casserole. For the quickest preparation, the noodles are cooked conventionally while the remainder of the dish is cooking in the microwave oven.

2½ cups uncooked noodles
(4 ounces)

1 pound ground veal

1 medium onion, chopped

1 clove garlic, minced

1 teaspoon natural meat
browning and seasoning
powder

⅔ cup water

½ tablespoon cornstarch

1 teaspoon instant beef
bouillon

½ teaspoon salt

½ teaspoon basil leaves

1 teaspoon Worcestershire
sauce

1 tablespoon chili sauce

Dash pepper

1 4-ounce can sliced
mushrooms, drained

1 10-ounce package frozen
Italian-cut green beans

2 tomatoes, coarsely chopped

1. Cook noodles as directed on package. Drain, rinse, and set aside.

2. Combine veal, onion, garlic, and browning powder in 2-quart microwave-safe casserole.

3. MICROWAVE (high), uncovered, 5–6 minutes or until no longer pink, stirring once. Stir in water, cornstarch, bouillon, salt, basil, Worcestershire sauce, chili sauce, and pepper; mix lightly. Cover with casserole lid.

4. MICROWAVE (high) 3–4 minutes or until mixture boils and thickens slightly, stirring once. Stir in noodles and mushrooms. Place beans on top. Cover.

5. MICROWAVE (high) 6–7 minutes or until beans are cooked. Stir in tomatoes. Cover.

6. MICROWAVE (high) 1½–2 minutes or until heated through.

TIPS

• Pork or turkey can be substituted for veal.

• If browning powder is not available, sprinkle meat with ¼ teaspoon paprika before microwaving.

• Individual servings can be frozen. To reheat, add 1 tablespoon water and microwave (high) 6–7 minutes, stirring once or twice.

LAMB STEW

**About 5 servings,
305 calories each**

Who says stew can't be lite? The extra vegetables add lots of flavor and color to this variation of a popular favorite.

1 pound cubed lean lamb

3 tablespoons flour

½ teaspoon salt

1 tablespoon cooking oil

1 medium onion, chopped

4 medium carrots, sliced (about 2 cups)

2 medium potatoes, cut into 1-inch pieces (about 2 cups)

2 ribs celery, sliced (about 1 cup)

1 cup water

1 bay leaf

½ teaspoon salt

½ teaspoon thyme leaves

1 teaspoon Worcestershire sauce

8 ounces fresh spinach, coarsely chopped

1. Coat lamb with flour and salt. Heat oil in shallow 2-quart pyroceramic casserole over medium-high heat on range. Add lamb and onion and brown on all sides, stirring occasionally. Stir in any remaining flour mixture. Add carrots, potatoes, celery, water, bay leaf, salt, thyme, and Worcestershire sauce; mix lightly. Cover with casserole lid.

2. MICROWAVE (high) 10 minutes; stir. Then, MICROWAVE (medium—50%) 15–20 minutes or until lamb and vegetables are tender, stirring once. Add spinach, mixing lightly.

3. MICROWAVE (high) 3–4 minutes or until spinach is tender. Remove bay leaf.

TIPS

● Lean pork can be substituted for lamb.

● If desired, add up to ¼ cup dry red wine for part of water.

● To use full power instead of medium power in step 2, use intervals of 5 minutes microwave and 5 minutes stand for the 15–20 minutes.

● Individual servings can be frozen. To reheat, add 1 tablespoon water and microwave (high) 5–6 minutes, stirring once or twice.

VEGETARIAN DELITE

**About 4 servings,
255 calories each**

*Layers of vegetables and bread crumbs are topped with a delicious mushroom sauce.
This dish is especially good served with fresh fruit.*

1 10-ounce package frozen
chopped spinach

1 small eggplant (about 1
pound)

1 teaspoon water

Salt

1 small onion, chopped

1 medium carrot, shredded
(about ½ cup)

1 tablespoon margarine

3 slices bread, crumbled

1 egg, slightly beaten

¾ cup (3 ounces) shredded Swiss
cheese

Salt

1 tablespoon cornflake crumbs

2 cups (8 ounces) sliced fresh
mushrooms

1 tablespoon margarine

¼ cup water

2 tablespoons dry white wine

1 teaspoon cornstarch

¼ teaspoon tarragon leaves

1. MICROWAVE (high) spinach in package (remove foil overwrap if necessary) 5–6 minutes or until hot, turning package over once. Drain and set aside.

2. Peel eggplant. Cut into 8 crosswise slices. Place 4 slices in bottom of 8-inch square microwave-safe baking dish. Add 1 teaspoon water and sprinkle with salt. Cover with plastic wrap.

3. MICROWAVE (high) 3–4 minutes or until eggplant is soft. Set aside. Combine onion, carrot, and margarine in 1-quart microwave-safe casserole.

4. MICROWAVE (high), uncovered, 4–5 minutes or until tender, stirring once. Mix in bread crumbs, egg, and ½ cup of the cheese. Stir in drained spinach. Spoon onto cooked eggplant. Top with remaining slices of eggplant. Sprinkle with salt and cornflake crumbs. Cover with plastic wrap.

5. MICROWAVE (high) 8–10 minutes or until eggplant is tender. Let stand covered. Combine mushrooms and 1 tablespoon margarine in 2-cup microwave-safe measure.

6. MICROWAVE (high), uncovered, 2–3 minutes or until tender. Add ¼ cup water, wine, cornstarch, and tarragon, mixing well.

7. MICROWAVE (high), uncovered, 1–2 minutes or until mixture boils and thickens, stirring once. Pour over eggplant; top with remaining ¼ cup cheese. Let stand until cheese is melted.

TIP

● Cheddar cheese can be substituted for Swiss.

ITALIAN PIE

**About 4 servings,
220 calories each**

This meatless combination of pasta, vegetables, and cheese will keep you coming back for more.

4 ounces uncooked linguine

1½ cups sliced zucchini (about 2 medium)

1 cup (4 ounces) sliced fresh mushrooms

1 egg, beaten

½ cup low-fat cottage cheese

1 8-ounce can tomato sauce

½ teaspoon oregano leaves

½ cup (2 ounces) shredded mozzarella cheese

1. Cook linguine as directed on package. Drain, rinse, and set aside.

2. Combine zucchini and mushrooms in 4-cup microwave-safe measure. Cover with plastic wrap.

3. MICROWAVE (high) 5–5½ minutes or until just about tender. Drain and set aside.

4. Combine linguine, egg, and cottage cheese in shallow 1½-quart microwave-safe casserole; mix lightly. Spread evenly over bottom of casserole. Top with zucchini mixture, spreading evenly. Mix together tomato sauce and oregano. Pour over zucchini. Cover with casserole lid.

5. MICROWAVE (high) 7–8 minutes or until hot (150°F), rotating casserole once. Sprinkle with cheese.

6. MICROWAVE (high), uncovered, 1–1½ minutes or until cheese is melted. Let stand about 5 minutes before cutting into wedges for serving.

TIPS

- An 8-inch microwave-safe pie plate can be substituted for casserole. Cover with plastic wrap in step 4.

- Spaghetti can be substituted for linguine.

- Individual servings can be frozen. To reheat, microwave (medium-high—70%) 5–6 minutes, rotating dish once.

CHAPTER
4
DISHES FOR ONE OR TWO

Cooking for one or two need not be a boring or time-consuming task. In fact, it can be a very creative time, especially with the microwave oven. The oven is often at its best when heating and cooking smaller quantities.

While this chapter contains recipes for two servings, many of the recipes are prepared in individual serving dishes, making them ideal for single servings as well. Just refrigerate or freeze one portion for another day. Or, invite a friend to come and share the meal.

In this section, you will find traditional favorites such as Italian Meatball Dinner and Hamburger Pie For Two, as well as more special-occasion dishes like Veal Parmigiana Dinner and Orange Roughy En Papillote.

If you frequently cook in small quantities, cook larger quantities of pasta and rice and freeze them in serving sizes to fit your needs. It only takes a minute or two to heat a serving of frozen rice or pasta in the microwave . . . much better than heating the large quantity of water each time or allowing for the slow simmering of rice. When the best buys are on larger can sizes or if smaller sizes are not available, remember that most foods can be frozen. Use what you need, package and freeze the remainder, and then use the microwave to thaw or heat for another meal.

For additional ideas for one or two, check the recipe "Tips" throughout the book. You can also use the larger quantity recipes, freezing extras in individual servings for quick reheats. Also, refer to chapter 8 on convenience foods, which includes a few recipes with just one or two servings.

With all the creative ideas in this section, you can eat tasty foods that are good for you, and yet not strain your food budget. Nothing is quite like a home-cooked meal, even when your needs are for only one or two servings.

CHICKEN CANNELLONI

**About 2 servings,
345 calories each**

*Flattened chicken breasts make the cannelloni-like wrappers for a creamy cheese filling.
The addition of noodles and broccoli transform this into a pretty one-dish meal for two.*

*1 cup uncooked noodles (about
2 ounces)*

*2 skinned and boned chicken
breasts (about 6 ounces)*

Garlic salt

¼ cup low-fat cottage cheese

*¼ cup shredded mozzarella
cheese*

1 green onion, sliced

*¼ teaspoon Italian seasoning or
basil leaves*

*1 cup fresh or frozen chopped
broccoli*

½ cup tomato sauce

*½ tablespoon grated Parmesan
cheese*

1. Cook noodles as directed on package. Drain, rinse, and set aside.

2. Flatten each chicken breast between plastic wrap until about ¼ inch thick. Sprinkle each lightly with garlic salt. Combine cottage cheese, mozzarella cheese, onion, and seasoning; mix well. Divide among chicken pieces, placing filling in center. Roll up with cheese inside. Place seam side down in shallow 1-quart microwave-safe baking dish. Cover with plastic wrap.

3. MICROWAVE (high) 3–4 minutes or until chicken is partially cooked. Arrange noodles and broccoli around rolls. Spoon tomato sauce over chicken. Cover with plastic wrap.

4. MICROWAVE (high) 3–4 minutes or until chicken is tender. Sprinkle with Parmesan cheese.

5. MICROWAVE (high), uncovered, 1½–2 minutes or until broccoli is tender.

LEMONY CHICKEN KABOBS

**About 2 servings,
350 calories each**

Start this recipe at least 2 hours ahead to allow ample time for the chicken to marinate.

**8 ounces skinned and boned
chicken breast**

1 tablespoon lemon juice

1 tablespoon honey

1 tablespoon soy sauce

¼ teaspoon garlic powder

⅔ cup quick-cooking rice

⅔ cup water

1 teaspoon parsley flakes

**½ teaspoon instant chicken
bouillon**

2 tablespoons water

1 teaspoon cornstarch

4 10-inch bamboo skewers

**1 small zucchini, cut into ½-inch
pieces**

4 cherry tomatoes

½ onion, cut into pieces

**¼ green pepper, cut into 1-inch
pieces**

1. Cut chicken into long thin strips. Combine lemon juice, honey, soy sauce, and garlic powder in 2-cup microwave-safe measure. Mix well; stir in chicken. Set aside to marinate for at least 2 hours.

2. Combine rice, ⅔ cup water, parsley, and bouillon in shallow 1-quart microwave-safe baking dish. Cover with lid or plastic wrap.

3. MICROWAVE (high) 3–4 minutes or until mixture boils. Set aside.

4. Remove chicken from marinade. Stir 2 tablespoons water and cornstarch into marinade.

5. MICROWAVE (high), uncovered, 1–1½ minutes or until mixture boils and thickens, stirring once. Set aside.

6. Fold chicken accordion-style and alternate on skewers with zucchini, tomatoes, onion, and green pepper. Place kabobs on rice. Spoon thickened marinade over kabobs. Cover with plastic wrap.

7. MICROWAVE (high) 4½–5½ minutes or until chicken is done, rotating dish once.

TIP

● About 1 cup cooked rice can be substituted for quick-cooking rice, water, and bouillon. Add parsley to rice before topping with kabobs.

MEXICAN CHICKEN OLE

About 2 servings, 350 calories each

Corn tortilla strips are mixed with chicken chunks and jicama in this south-of-the-border fare for two.

1 small onion, chopped

1 tablespoon margarine

1 tablespoon flour

¾ cup skim milk

¼ teaspoon salt

2 corn tortillas (about 6-inch size)

1 cup cubed cooked chicken

2 tablespoons diced mild green chilies

½ cup peeled cubed jicama

2 tablespoons shredded cheddar cheese

1 small tomato, chopped

1 tablespoon sliced ripe olives

1. Combine onion and margarine in shallow 1-quart microwave-safe casserole.

2. MICROWAVE (high), uncovered, 1½–2 minutes or until onion is just about tender. Stir in flour until blended. Gradually add milk and salt, mixing well.

3. MICROWAVE (high), uncovered, 2–3 minutes or until mixture boils and thickens, stirring twice. Cut tortillas into ½-inch strips. Add to sauce along with chicken, chilies, jicama, and cheese; mix lightly.

4. MICROWAVE (high), uncovered, 3–4 minutes or until heated through. Top with tomato and olives.

CHICKEN CHOW MEIN

**About 2 servings,
265 calories each**

This recipe is so quick and easy that chow mein lovers will want to make it often. You will be pleased at the generous servings for so few calories.

1 cup sliced celery

1 medium onion, chopped

1 cup cubed cooked chicken

1 cup water

1 8-ounce can sliced water chestnuts, drained

1½ tablespoons cornstarch

½ tablespoon instant chicken bouillon

1 tablespoon diced pimiento

1 tablespoon soy sauce

½ cup chow mein noodles

1. Combine celery and onion in 1-quart microwave-safe casserole. Cover with casserole lid.

2. MICROWAVE (high) 1½–2 minutes or until partially cooked. Stir in remaining ingredients except noodles. Cover.

3. MICROWAVE (high) 4½–5½ minutes or until mixture boils and thickens, stirring once. Sprinkle with noodles.

4. MICROWAVE (high), uncovered, 1–1½ minutes or until noodles are heated.

TIPS

• A 4-ounce can sliced mushrooms, drained, can be substituted for water chestnuts.

• To use uncooked chicken, add 4 ounces boneless breast to vegetables in step 1. Increase cooking time in step 2 to 3–4 minutes. Cut chicken into pieces and add with remaining ingredients.

MEXICAN ENCHILADAS

About 2 servings, 335 calories each

A mixture of chicken and vegetables is rolled inside corn tortillas in this Mexican favorite.

1 small tomato, quartered

1 clove garlic, minced

2 tablespoons chopped onion

¾ cup shredded zucchini (about 1 medium)

½ cup sliced fresh mushrooms

1 cup finely chopped cooked chicken

⅓ cup shredded Monterey Jack cheese with hot peppers

½ teaspoon chili powder

⅛ teaspoon salt

4 corn tortillas (about 6-inch size)

1 cup chopped lettuce

1. Chop three of the tomato quarters (reserve other quarter). Combine chopped tomato, garlic, onion, zucchini, and mushrooms in 1-quart microwave-safe casserole. Cover with casserole lid.

2. MICROWAVE (high) 5–6 minutes or until vegetables are tender, stirring once or twice. Stir in chicken, cheese, chili powder, and salt.

3. Spoon a scant ½ cup chicken mixture onto each tortilla. Roll up with filling inside. Arrange in 10- by 6-inch microwave-safe baking dish. Cover with waxed paper.

4. MICROWAVE (high) 3–3½ minutes or until heated through, rotating dish once. Sprinkle with lettuce. Chop remaining tomato and sprinkle over lettuce.

TIPS

● If using regular Jack cheese, add a few drops hot pepper sauce or a tablespoon diced green chilies.

● Other cooked meat can be substituted for chicken.

● Flour tortillas can be substituted. Calories will be slightly higher.

STUFFED EGGPLANT SUPREME

**About 2 servings,
345 calories each**

*Eggplant lovers will want to try this easy main dish. Turkey, rice, and mushrooms make
the tasty stuffing for the eggplant halves.*

½ **pound ground turkey**

¼ **cup chopped green pepper**

⅛ **teaspoon garlic powder**

1 **small eggplant (about 1
pound)**

1 **cup (4 ounces) sliced fresh
mushrooms**

½ **cup quick-cooking rice**

¼ **cup catsup**

¼ **teaspoon salt**

⅛ **teaspoon oregano leaves**

2 **tablespoons grated Parmesan
cheese**

1. Crumble turkey into 1-quart microwave-safe
casserole. Add green pepper and garlic powder.

2. MICROWAVE (high), uncovered, 3–4 minutes or
until no longer pink, stirring once. Drain and set
aside.

3. Cut eggplant in half vertically; scoop out center,
leaving ¼-inch-thick shells. Place shells on
microwave-safe serving plate. Set aside. Chop
the scooped-out eggplant; add to turkey mixture.
Mix in mushrooms, rice, catsup, salt, and
oregano. Cover with casserole lid.

4. MICROWAVE (high) 5–6 minutes or until
vegetables are just about tender, stirring once.
Spoon mixture into eggplant shells. Sprinkle
with Parmesan cheese. Cover with plastic wrap.

5. MICROWAVE (high) 7–8 minutes or until shells
are tender, rotating plate once.

TIP

● Often a 1-pound package of frozen ground turkey can be cut in half with a sharp
knife. To thaw and cook the frozen turkey, microwave (high) 2–2½ minutes, stirring
once. Add green pepper and garlic and microwave 3–4 minutes. Wrap the frozen
portion and return it to the freezer.

COLORFUL COD DINNER

**About 2 servings,
220 calories each**

Potato, cod, and broccoli cook together in this gourmet dinner for two.

1 medium potato

4 ounces fresh broccoli (about 2 cups)

8 ounces cod or torsk

⅛ teaspoon garlic salt

½ cup sliced fresh mushrooms

½ tablespoon dry sherry (optional)

⅛ teaspoon tarragon leaves

1 teaspoon margarine

2 slices lemon

2 tablespoons pasteurized process cheese spread (Cheez Whiz)

Salt and pepper

1. Prick potato with fork. Place on paper towel in microwave oven.

2. MICROWAVE (high) 4–5 minutes or until just about tender, turning potato over once. Set aside.

3. Cut broccoli into spears about 2 inches long and ½ inch thick. Arrange broccoli down center of 8-inch round microwave-safe baking dish. Cover with plastic wrap.

4. MICROWAVE (high) 1½–2 minutes or until hot. Cut cod into serving pieces. Place on broccoli. Sprinkle with garlic salt; top with mushrooms, sherry, tarragon, margarine, and lemon slices. Cut potato in half lengthwise. Press on sides to fluff potato. Arrange next to broccoli on either side of dish. Spoon cheese spread onto potato; sprinkle with salt and pepper. Cover with plastic wrap.

5. MICROWAVE (high) 4–5 minutes or until fish flakes apart easily with fork and broccoli is tender.

ORANGE ROUGHY EN PAPILLOTE

**About 2 servings,
215 calories each**

Fish fillets and savory vegetables are microwaved to perfection in their own individual parchment envelopes.

2 small potatoes

Parchment paper

½ pound orange roughy

Salt

Paprika

1 small carrot

1 small zucchini

½ cup whole mushrooms

¼ teaspoon dill weed

1 tablespoon margarine

2 lemon slices

1. Prick potatoes with fork. Place on paper towel in microwave oven.

2. MICROWAVE (high) 3–4 minutes or until soft, turning potatoes over once.

3. Cut two pieces of parchment paper about 15- by 20-inches. Divide fish between the two pieces of paper. Sprinkle with salt and paprika. Cut each potato into 4 slices and place on fish. Cut carrot and zucchini into matchstick pieces, about 2 inches long, and divide between the two servings. Add mushrooms to each serving; sprinkle with dill. Place a piece of margarine on top of each serving. Bring 20-inch sides of paper to center and make a double fold. Fold up ends and tuck underneath. Place on microwave-safe serving plate.

4. MICROWAVE (high) 5–6 minutes or until fish flakes apart easily with fork. Let stand 5 minutes. Open packets and top each with a lemon slice.

TIPS

- If parchment paper is not available, prepare individual servings on microwave-safe plates. Cover with plastic wrap.

- Other favorite fish fillets can be substituted.

CHEESY CRAB AND BROCCOLI CASSEROLES

About 2 servings, 295 calories each

Frozen broccoli in cheese sauce is combined with crabmeat to make a quick filling for individual rice shells.

½ cup water

½ cup quick-cooking rice

⅛ teaspoon salt

1 10-ounce package frozen broccoli in cheese sauce

1 egg, slightly beaten

1 6-ounce package frozen crabmeat, thawed and drained

¼ teaspoon tarragon leaves

1 tablespoon dry white wine

1 tablespoon diced pimiento

3–5 drops hot pepper sauce

Lemon wedges (optional)

1. MICROWAVE (high) water in uncovered 2-cup microwave-safe measure 1½–2 minutes or until boiling. Add rice and salt. Let stand 5 minutes. Make a small slit in broccoli pouch to allow steam to escape. Place pouch in microwave oven.

2. MICROWAVE (high) 6–7 minutes or until hot. Mix egg with rice. Divide mixture between two 10- or 16-ounce microwave-safe individual baking dishes. Press rice against bottom and up sides of dishes; set aside.

3. Combine crabmeat, tarragon, wine, pimiento, and pepper sauce. Mix in broccoli. Spoon into rice shells.

4. MICROWAVE (high), uncovered, 4–5 minutes or until heated through, rearranging dishes once. If desired, serve with lemon wedges.

TIPS

- Cut-up imitation crabmeat sticks can be substituted for frozen crabmeat. Or, use a 6-ounce can crab, rinsed and drained.

- If omitting wine, add ¼ teaspoon lemon juice.

VERMICELLI WITH SHRIMP AND VEGETABLES

About 2 servings, 340 calories each

Shrimp, pasta, and vegetables are glazed with a creamy sauce. Slices of fruit and French bread would complement the dish nicely.

3 cups hot water

¼ teaspoon salt

2 ounces uncooked vermicelli, broken in half

2 cups frozen vegetable combination (broccoli, cauliflower, and carrots)

1 ounce cream cheese (2 tablespoons)

½ cup skim milk

¼ teaspoon salt

¼ teaspoon basil leaves

6 ounces frozen cooked shrimp, thawed and rinsed

2 tablespoons grated Parmesan cheese

Snipped fresh parsley

1. Combine water and ¼ teaspoon salt in 2-quart microwave-safe mixing bowl.

2. MICROWAVE (high), uncovered, 5–6 minutes or until boiling. Add vermicelli and mix with fork.

3. MICROWAVE (high), uncovered, 5–6 minutes or until tender. Drain, rinse, and set aside. Place frozen vegetables in 1-quart microwave-safe casserole. Cover with casserole lid.

4. MICROWAVE (high) 6–7 minutes or until tender. Add cream cheese; mix with vegetables until softened. Stir in milk, ¼ teaspoon salt, basil, shrimp, and vermicelli. Sprinkle with Parmesan cheese.

5. MICROWAVE (high), uncovered, 2–3 minutes or until heated through (150°F). Sprinkle with parsley.

TIPS

● Other cooked seafood or poultry can be substituted for shrimp.

● If substituting spaghetti for vermicelli, increase cooking time in step 3 to 8–9 minutes.

INDIVIDUAL ZUCCHINI PIES

**About 2 servings,
310 calories each**

*Sliced zucchini makes the easy crust, and tuna and stuffing mix make the tasty filling for
these individual entrees.*

2 cups sliced zucchini (about 2
  medium)

½ cup chopped celery

1 small onion, chopped

1 tablespoon margarine

¾ cup dry herb-seasoned
  stuffing mix

1 6½-ounce can water-packed
  tuna, drained

1 egg, slightly beaten

2 tablespoons skim milk

⅛ teaspoon basil leaves

Dash pepper

1 small tomato, chopped

1. Divide zucchini between two 12- or 16-ounce individual serving dishes. Cover with plastic wrap.

2. MICROWAVE (high) 2½–3 minutes or until just about tender. Set aside. Combine celery, onion, and margarine in 4-cup microwave-safe measure.

3. MICROWAVE (high), uncovered, 1½–2 minutes or until just about tender. Stir in stuffing, tuna, egg, milk, basil, and pepper. Arrange zucchini in single layer over bottom and up sides of dishes. Spoon tuna mixture into each dish. Cover with plastic wrap.

4. MICROWAVE (high) 3–4 minutes or until heated through. Top with tomato.

5. MICROWAVE (high), uncovered, 1½–2 minutes or until tomato is warm.

BEEF ANOTHER TIME

**About 2 servings,
290 calories each**

Yes, this meat and potato casserole is light and really quite low in calories.

1 small onion, chopped

½ cup sliced fresh mushrooms

½ cup skim milk

½ tablespoon flour

⅛ teaspoon salt

¾ cup cubed cooked beef

1 cup frozen peas and carrots

1 cup prepared mashed potatoes

2 tablespoons shredded cheddar cheese

1. Combine onion and mushrooms in 1-quart microwave-safe casserole. Cover with casserole lid.

2. MICROWAVE (high) 2–3 minutes or until just about tender. Stir in milk, flour, and salt until blended. Add beef and peas and carrots.

3. MICROWAVE (high), uncovered, 4–5 minutes or until mixture boils and thickens, stirring once or twice. Spoon potatoes by rounded teaspoonful onto meat mixture.

4. MICROWAVE (high), uncovered, 2–3 minutes or until potatoes are heated. Sprinkle with cheese. Let stand a few minutes before serving.

TIPS

● If you do not have leftover mashed potatoes, prepare using instant variety.

● Cheese can be omitted; sprinkle potatoes with paprika before heating in step **4**.

ITALIAN MEATBALL DINNER

About 2 servings, 340 calories each

Meatballs, vegetables, and pasta . . . just right for two.

2 ounces uncooked linguine

½ pound extra-lean ground beef

2 tablespoons quick-cooking rolled oats

1 tablespoon grated Parmesan cheese

½ teaspoon onion salt

Dash pepper

1 clove garlic, minced

1 cup frozen vegetable combination (green beans, broccoli, and mushrooms)

½ cup sliced fresh mushrooms

1 8-ounce can tomato sauce

¼ teaspoon oregano leaves

¼ teaspoon sugar

1. Cook linguine as directed on package. Drain, rinse, and set aside.

2. Combine ground beef, oats, cheese, salt, and pepper; mix well. Form into six meatballs. Arrange in 8-inch microwave-safe pie plate or shallow casserole.

3. MICROWAVE (high), uncovered, 3–3½ minutes or until no longer pink, rearranging once. Drain and set aside. Combine garlic, frozen vegetables, and mushrooms in 2-cup microwave-safe measure. Cover with plastic wrap.

4. MICROWAVE (high) 3–3½ minutes or until tender-crisp. Stir in tomato sauce, oregano, and sugar. Move meatballs to one side of pie plate. Add linguine and place meatballs on top. Spoon tomato sauce mixture over meatballs.

5. MICROWAVE (high), uncovered, 4–5 minutes or until heated through (150°F).

HAMBURGER PIE FOR TWO

**About 2 servings,
305 calories each**

You'll like the flavors of this home-style favorite. See the recipe Tips for using leftover mashed potatoes.

½ **cup water**

¼ **teaspoon salt**

2 **tablespoons skim milk**

½ **cup instant potato flakes or
granules**

½ **pound lean ground beef**

1 **medium onion, chopped**

½ **cup sliced celery**

¾ **cup sliced carrot (1 medium)**

1 **tablespoon flour**

1 **teaspoon instant beef bouillon**

⅛ **teaspoon salt**

Dash pepper

1 **cup water**

½ **teaspoon parsley flakes**

1. Combine ½ cup water and ¼ teaspoon salt in 2-cup microwave-safe measure.
2. MICROWAVE (high), uncovered, 1½–2 minutes or until mixture boils. Stir in milk and potato flakes with fork. Set aside.
3. Crumble ground beef into 1-quart microwave-safe casserole. Add onion, celery, and carrot.
4. MICROWAVE (high), uncovered, 3–4 minutes or until meat is no longer pink, stirring once. Drain. Stir in flour, bouillon, ⅛ teaspoon salt, pepper, and 1 cup water.
5. MICROWAVE (high), uncovered, 4–5 minutes or until mixture boils and thickens, stirring once. Spoon potatoes by rounded teaspoonful onto meat mixture. Sprinkle with parsley flakes.
6. MICROWAVE (high), uncovered, 1½–2 minutes or until heated through.

TIPS

- Leftover mashed potatoes can be substituted for first four ingredients, using about ¾ cup. If cold, increase time in step 6 to 2–3 minutes.

- About 1 cup cubed cooked beef can be substituted for ground beef. Add 1 tablespoon water to vegetables in step 3 and add beef with water in step 4.

SQUASH BLOSSOMS

**About 2 servings,
345 calories each**

Mexican-flavored meat patties cook in the center of acorn squash slices. They look like blossoms in a bed of broccoli.

1 small acorn squash (about 1 pound)

½ pound lean ground beef

¼ cup quick-cooking rolled oats

3 tablespoons picante sauce

1 teaspoon instant minced onion

½ teaspoon salt

⅛ teaspoon pepper

1 cup fresh or frozen broccoli pieces

2 tablespoons shredded Monterey Jack cheese

1. Prick squash with fork several times. Place on paper towel in microwave oven.

2. MICROWAVE (high) 6–8 minutes or until just about tender, turning squash over once. Set aside.

3. Combine ground beef, oats, 2 tablespoons of the picante sauce, minced onion, salt, and pepper; mix well.

4. Cut squash in half crosswise. Scoop out seeds. Place halves cut side up in 10- by 6-inch microwave-safe baking dish. Divide meat mixture between squash halves, heaping mixture into center. Top with remaining 1 tablespoon picante sauce. Place broccoli in dish around squash. Cover with plastic wrap.

5. MICROWAVE (high) 6–7 minutes or until meat is done and broccoli is tender, rotating dish once. Sprinkle meat with cheese.

6. MICROWAVE (high), uncovered, 1–1½ minutes or until cheese is melted.

TIPS

- If a small squash is not available, use a larger one and increase time in step 2 accordingly. Cut off one slice from each end and use in this recipe. Refrigerate or freeze remainder for another day.

- If necessary, slice a little off the pointed end of squash to allow it to stand upright in dish.

PORK CHOPS WITH CREOLE RICE   About 2 servings, 335 calories each

Tender pork chops simmer with flavorful rice in this easy entree.

¼ **cup chopped green pepper**

1 **green onion, sliced (including top)**

1 **teaspoon margarine**

¼ **cup uncooked long-grain rice**

½ **cup water**

1 **small tomato, chopped**

¼ **teaspoon salt**

2 **boneless pork chops (about 6 ounces)**

1 **tablespoon chili sauce**

1. Combine green pepper, onion, and margarine in shallow 1-quart microwave-safe casserole.

2. MICROWAVE (high), uncovered, 2–3 minutes or until vegetables are partially cooked. Add rice, water, tomato, and salt. Cover with casserole lid.

3. MICROWAVE (high) 5–6 minutes or until mixture boils. Brush both sides of pork chops with chili sauce. Place on rice. Cover.

4. MICROWAVE (low—30%) 25–35 minutes or until liquid is absorbed. Let stand about 5 minutes before serving.

TIPS

● When fresh tomatoes are less flavorful and juicy, add 1 tablespoon catsup or chili sauce for additional flavor.

● Chops can be sprinkled with natural browning and seasoning powder rather than brushed with chili sauce.

● To use full power instead of low power in step 4, use intervals of 3 minutes microwave and 5 minutes stand for the 25–35 minutes.

SAVORY PORK ROLL-UPS

**About 2 servings,
295 calories each**

*Herb-seasoned stuffing is tucked inside tender rolls of pork. Japanese-style vegetables
complete this one-dish meal.*

¼ *cup chopped celery*

2 *tablespoons chopped onion*

1 *clove garlic, minced*

1 *tablespoon margarine*

½ *cup dry herb-seasoned
stuffing cubes*

3 *tablespoons water*

8 *ounces pork tenderloin patties*

2 *cups frozen Japanese-style
vegetables*

¼ *teaspoon garlic salt*

Paprika

Water

½ *tablespoon cornstarch*

1. Combine celery, onion, garlic, and margarine in 8-inch round microwave-safe baking dish.

2. MICROWAVE (high), uncovered, 2–3 minutes or until partially cooked. Mix in stuffing cubes and water; set aside. Flatten each pork patty, if necessary, to about ¼-inch thickness. Divide stuffing mixture among meat patties. Roll up and fasten with toothpick. Place frozen vegetables in the round baking dish; top with pork rolls. Sprinkle with garlic salt and paprika. Cover with plastic wrap.

3. MICROWAVE (high) 6–7 minutes or until meat and vegetables are tender, rotating dish once. Drain juices into 1-cup microwave-safe measure. Add water to make ½ cup. Stir in cornstarch until smooth.

4. MICROWAVE (high), uncovered, 1½–2 minutes or until mixture boils and thickens, stirring once. Spoon over meat.

TIP

● If pork tenderloin patties are not available, use 8 ounces pork tenderloin, cut into four pieces and flattened to ¼-inch thickness.

SMOKED CHOPS AND KRAUT

About 2 servings, 340 calories each

Sauerkraut is light on calories but adds a lot of flavor to a combination like this.

2 smoked pork chops (about 6 ounces)

1 16-ounce can sauerkraut, drained, rinsed, and squeezed

1 medium apple, chopped

2 tablespoons chopped onion

½ tablespoon brown sugar

⅛ teaspoon caraway seed

¼ cup water

1 large potato (about 8 ounces)

Parsley flakes (optional)

1. Trim fat from chops. Place chops in 10- by 6-inch microwave-safe baking dish. Top with sauerkraut, apple, onion, brown sugar, and caraway; mix lightly without disturbing chops. Add water. Scrub potato and cut in half lengthwise. Place cut side down on sauerkraut at each end of dish. Cover with plastic wrap.

2. MICROWAVE (medium-high—70%) 14–16 minutes or until chops and potato are tender, rotating dish once. Sprinkle with parsley.

TIPS

- To use full power instead of medium-high power in step 2, microwave 6 minutes, let stand 3 minutes, rotate dish, and microwave 5–7 minutes.

- These servings of sauerkraut are very generous. If you prefer smaller servings, save leftovers for another meal with pork chops or smoked sausages; just prepare the recipe using half the quantity of sauerkraut.

HAM-VEGETABLE BAKE

About 2 servings, 220 calories each

Ham, potatoes, and frozen vegetables are combined with Swiss cheese in this lower-calorie entree.

¼ cup chopped green pepper

2 green onions, sliced (including tops)

1 tablespoon margarine

½ 12-ounce package frozen hash browns (2 patties)

1 cup cubed lean ham (about 4 ounces)

1 cup frozen vegetable combination (broccoli, cauliflower, and carrots)

½ teaspoon seasoned salt

¼ cup shredded Swiss cheese

1. Combine green pepper, onions, and margarine in 1-quart microwave-safe casserole.

2. MICROWAVE (high), uncovered, 2–3 minutes or until tender. Add hash browns. Cover with casserole lid.

3. MICROWAVE (high) 3–4 minutes or until hash browns are thawed. Mix in ham, vegetables, and seasoned salt. Cover.

4. MICROWAVE (high) 4–5 minutes or until vegetables are tender. Sprinkle with cheese. Cover and let stand about 5 minutes before serving.

VEAL PARMIGIANA DINNER

About 2 servings, 340 calories each

You will surely enjoy this appealing main dish combining breaded veal cutlets with noodles and vegetables. Note in the recipe Tips that you can also enjoy it prepared with pork.

2 ounces uncooked fettuccini, broken in half

2 tablespoons grated Parmesan cheese

1 tablespoon flour

6 ounces thinly sliced veal

Paprika

2 tablespoons catsup

¼ teaspoon onion powder

2 tablespoons water

1 medium zucchini, sliced (about 1 cup)

1 small tomato, chopped

½ cup sliced fresh mushrooms

Dash thyme

Parsley flakes

2 tablespoons shredded mozzarella cheese

1. Cook fettuccini as directed on package. Drain, rinse, and set aside.

2. Combine Parmesan cheese and flour on waxed paper; mix well. Coat veal with mixture. Roll up meat and place seam side down near sides of 8-inch round microwave-safe baking dish. Sprinkle with paprika. Combine catsup, onion powder, and water; mix well and pour over meat. Place zucchini, tomato, and mushrooms in center of dish. Sprinkle with thyme. Cover with plastic wrap.

3. MICROWAVE (medium—50%) 9–11 minutes or until meat is tender. Push meat to center of dish. Add fettuccini to outer part of dish. Sprinkle with parsley. Sprinkle meat and vegetables with mozzarella cheese.

4. MICROWAVE (high), uncovered, 1–2 minutes or until heated through.

TIPS

- Sliced lean pork can be substituted for veal.

- Other vegetable combinations or other pastas can be substituted. Or, use 1½ cups of favorite frozen vegetable combination.

- To use full power instead of medium power in step 3, use intervals of 3 minutes microwave and 3 minutes stand for the 9–11 minutes.

VEGETABLE CASSEROLES

About 2 servings, 315 calories each

These individual dishes are lite, yet satisfying meatless main dishes.

½ cup water

½ cup quick-cooking rice

4 ounces torn fresh spinach (about 4 cups)

1 medium carrot, shredded (about ½ cup)

3 green onions, sliced (including tops)

1 tablespoon margarine

1 egg, slightly beaten

½ cup (2 ounces) shredded cheddar cheese

¼ teaspoon seasoned salt

1. MICROWAVE (high) water in uncovered 2-cup microwave-safe measure 1½–2 minutes or until boiling. Stir in rice; set aside. Combine spinach, carrot, onions, and margarine in 1-quart microwave-safe casserole. Cover with casserole lid.

2. MICROWAVE (high) 3½–4 minutes or until carrot is tender. Mix in rice, egg, cheese, and seasoned salt. Divide evenly between two 10-ounce microwave-safe baking dishes.

3. MICROWAVE (high), uncovered, 4–5 minutes or until center is set, rearranging dishes once.

TIPS

• If desired, substitute half of a 10-ounce package, partially thawed, frozen chopped spinach for fresh spinach.

• Casserole mixture can remain in 1-quart casserole for heating as directed in step 3.

CHAPTER
5
SPECIAL OCCASION DISHES

Friends are coming for dinner or you are celebrating a special honor or occasion with your family. What a perfect opportunity for something a little extra special. Special occasions need not mean lots of dishes and long hours in the kitchen. The recipes in this section will show you how effortless special can be. And, perhaps best of all, they show how food can taste especially good without being laden with extra calories.

Some of the recipes in this section may seem a little long, but they're really not when you consider that each recipe includes a protein item as well as a vegetable and a starch. Since the foods are arranged on one common serving plate, the serving and clean-up are simple. To save on last minute preparation, make the dishes up to one hour before serving. Then, just increase the final heating time to bring all parts to serving temperature. This gives you plenty of time to get ready for your guests and wash any preparation dishes. Also, preparation steps such as chopping, measuring, and assembling can be done even earlier in the day.

An attractive table enhances any meal. Use time early in the day to set the table, including centerpiece and serving pieces. Use colors that enhance the colors of the food included in your special occasion main dish.

Most recipes in this section serve four to eight, so you will find a size to fit most of your special occasion needs. Larger quantity recipes were not included since the amount of food becomes too great to fit on a single serving plate and heat efficiently in the microwave oven.

A large microwave-safe serving plate is often needed to assemble, heat, and serve the food. If you have a full-size oven, you can use up to a 12-inch round plate. If your oven is smaller, you will need to adjust the size downward. Some ovens will accommodate a larger oval plate better than they will a round plate. If you do not have such a plate, you may want to invest in a versatile one that will fit inside your oven for occasions such as these. The platters from many dinnerware sets are useable as long as the dish is microwaveable. Just be sure there is no metal trim on the dish and that the dish will withstand the heat from the food. A large rectangular baking dish is another option if you do not have a large plate or platter.

The order of preparation in each recipe takes into account the cooking and standing times required. Foods that retain heat best and reheat easiest are usually prepared first. Also, foods that need standing time before slicing, such as roasts, are best prepared early.

Once all the components of a dish are assembled, the dish is heated a few minutes longer to assure that all foods are at serving temperature.

Several recipes in this section include roasts. Generally, we have used smaller-size roasts, but even so, there will often be leftovers. These make excellent sandwiches the next day, or use extras in some of the other recipes in this book calling for cooked meat. Caesar's Beef Salad and Beef Another Time are examples of recipes using cooked beef. Quick Linguine Delite, Chicken-Potato Bake, and Tex-Mex Chicken Tacos use cooked chicken. If you have leftover cooked pork, use it for Pork and Noodles.

When you have extra servings of these special occasion recipes, check the recipe "Tips" for information on freezing individual servings. They are great "planned overs" for busy days when there is just time to reheat.

Whatever the occasion or celebration, the dishes in this section will add a special festive touch, yet help you maintain balanced and nutritious meals. Page through the chapter and note the variety of recipes. Find a recipe to suit your occasion or, better yet, find a special occasion to celebrate while you enjoy some of the many attractive, great-tasting food combinations here.

ALOHA CHICKEN SALAD

**About 6 servings,
330 calories each**

A taste of the tropics, served in fresh pineapple boats. Add crusty rolls or bread sticks for a special lunch or brunch.

1 pound skinned and boned chicken breasts

1 ripe fresh pineapple (about 5 pounds)

½ cup finely chopped celery

½ cup shredded carrot (1 medium)

⅓ cup macadamia nuts

½ cup plain yogurt

1 tablespoon mayonnaise or salad dressing

1 teaspoon brown sugar

¼ teaspoon cinnamon

¼ cup flaked coconut

1 teaspoon water

1. Place chicken in shallow baking dish. Cover with waxed paper.

2. MICROWAVE (medium-high—70%) 7–9 minutes or until chicken is done. Cool enough to handle.

3. Cut pineapple in half lengthwise, cutting through leafy top. Cut each half into three wedges, again cutting through top. Carefully cut pineapple from shell, leaving about ¼ inch fruit on shell. Cut off core and discard. Cut pineapple into chunks and place in bowl. Add celery, carrot, nuts, yogurt, mayonnaise, brown sugar, and cinnamon to pineapple; mix lightly. Refrigerate until served. Cut chicken into bite-size pieces. Add to salad just before serving; mix lightly and spoon into pineapple shells.

4. Combine coconut and water in 5-ounce microwave-safe custard cup.

5. MICROWAVE (high), uncovered, 2–2½ minutes or until lightly toasted, stirring 3 or 4 times. Cool and sprinkle over salads just before serving.

TIPS

- To use full power instead of medium-high power in step 2, microwave 4 minutes, let stand 3 minutes, rotate dish, and microwave 2–3 minutes.

- About 3 cups cubed cooked chicken, turkey, ham, or a combination can be used.

SAUTEED CHICKEN BREAST WITH ARTICHOKES

**About 6 servings,
340 calories each**

Chicken breasts are sautéed in garlic butter and then combined with carrots, artichoke hearts and rice for this meal-in-a-dish.

- **1 5-ounce package brown and wild rice mix**
- **⅔ cup uncooked long-grain rice**
- **2¼ cups water**
- **6 medium carrots, sliced (about 3 cups)**
- **1 9-ounce package frozen artichoke hearts**
- **2 tablespoons water**
- **2 tablespoons margarine**
- **⅛ teaspoon tarrragon leaves**
- **1½ pounds skinned and boned chicken breasts**
- **3 green onions, sliced (including tops)**
- **2 cloves garlic, minced**
- **2 teaspoons instant chicken bouillon**
- **1 tablespoon flour**
- **¼ cup water**
- **3 tablespoons dry white wine**

1. Combine rice packets from mix, long-grain rice, and water in 1½-quart microwave-safe casserole. Cover with casserole lid.

2. MICROWAVE (high) 7–8 minutes or until mixture boils. Then, MICROWAVE (low—30%) 16–20 minutes or until tender. Set aside.

3. Combine carrots, artichoke hearts, and 2 tablespoons water in 1-quart microwave-safe casserole. Cover with casserole lid.

4. MICROWAVE (high) 10–12 minutes or until carrots are just about tender, stirring once. Drain; add 1 tablespoon of the margarine and tarragon. Mix lightly and set aside.

5. Heat remaining 1 tablespoon margarine in shallow 1½-quart pyroceramic casserole over medium-high heat on range. Add chicken breasts; brown on both sides. Add green onions, garlic, and bouillon. Combine flour, ¼ cup water, and wine; blend until smooth. Stir into chicken. Cover with casserole lid.

6. MICROWAVE (medium-high—70%) 8–10 minutes or until chicken is tender, stirring once. Spoon rice into center of large microwave-safe plate. Top with chicken breasts and sauce. Arrange carrots and artichoke hearts around rice.

7. MICROWAVE (high), uncovered, 4–6 minutes or until heated through.

TIP

- To use full power instead of low power in step 2, use intervals of 2 minutes microwave and 5 minutes stand for the 16–20 minutes. In step 6, microwave 6–8 minutes, stirring twice.

CHICKEN ROLLS WITH VEGETABLES SUPREME

About 4 servings, 220 calories each

Spaghetti squash makes the base for this interesting combination of chicken and vegetables.

1 medium spaghetti squash

1½ cups sliced carrots (about 3 medium)

1 tablespoon water

1 tablespoon margarine

¼ teaspoon tarragon leaves

4 small skinned and boned chicken breasts (about 12 ounces)

Seasoned salt

2 teaspoons snipped chives

1 tablespoon grated Parmesan cheese

¼ teaspoon paprika

1 8-ounce package frozen asparagus spears

1. Prick squash several times with fork. Place on paper towel in microwave oven.

2. MICROWAVE (high) 12–14 minutes or until just about tender, turning squash over once. Set aside. Combine carrots and water in 2-cup microwave-safe measure. Cover with plastic wrap.

3. MICROWAVE (high) 3½–4 minutes or until partially cooked. Drain. Add margarine and tarragon; mix lightly. Set aside covered.

4. Flatten each chicken breast by placing between plastic wrap and pounding with rolling pin until ¼ inch thick. Sprinkle each with seasoned salt and ½ teaspoon chives. Roll up. Combine Parmesan cheese and paprika on waxed paper. Coat each chicken breast with mixture.

5. Cut squash in half crosswise; remove seeds. Unwind spaghetti-like strands from squash with fork; place on large microwave-safe serving plate. Spoon the carrots into the center of the dish; arrange chicken rolls near edge of dish.

6. MICROWAVE (high) asparagus in package (remove foil overwrap if necessary) 2–3 minutes or until partially thawed. Arrange asparagus spoke-fashion among the chicken rolls. Cover with plastic wrap.

7. MICROWAVE (high) 10–12 minutes or until chicken is done, rotating dish once.

TIP

● About 4 ounces spaghetti, cooked as directed on package, can be substituted for spaghetti squash. Drain, rinse, and arrange on serving plate before adding other ingredients.

CHICKEN RISOTTO

**About 4 servings,
350 calories each**

A savory mushroom-sherry sauce tops chicken breasts and asparagus served on a bed of rice.

⅔ **cup uncooked long-grain rice**

1⅓ **cups water**

1 **8-ounce package frozen asparagus spears**

2 **whole chicken breasts, skinned and split**

Paprika

1 **cup (4 ounces) sliced fresh mushrooms**

Water

2 **teaspoons cornstarch**

2 **teaspoons instant chicken bouillon**

¼ **teaspoon salt**

2 **tablespoons dry sherry (optional)**

3 **tablespoons plain yogurt**

1. Combine rice and 1⅓ cups water in 12- by 8-inch microwave-safe baking dish. Cover with waxed paper.

2. MICROWAVE (high) 9–10 minutes or until steaming hot. Separate frozen asparagus spears and arrange in single layer on rice. Place chicken breasts bone side down on asparagus. Sprinkle chicken with paprika. Cover with waxed paper.

3. MICROWAVE (high) 20–25 minutes or until chicken and rice are tender, rotating dish once. Set aside covered.

4. Place mushrooms in 4-cup microwave-safe measure; cover with plastic wrap.

5. MICROWAVE (high), 2–2½ minutes or until mushrooms are tender, stirring once. Add water to make 1 cup. Stir in cornstarch; mix well. Stir in bouillon, salt, and sherry.

6. MICROWAVE (high), uncovered, 2–3 minutes or until mixture boils and thickens, stirring once. Stir in yogurt. Spoon sauce over chicken.

TIPS

● If frozen asparagus does not separate easily, microwave 1–2 minutes.

● About 1 pound fresh asparagus, washed and trimmed, can be substituted for frozen.

● Individual servings can be frozen. To reheat, microwave (medium-high—70%) 5–6 minutes.

ITALIAN CHICKEN ON NOODLES

About 4 servings, 350 calories each

Spinach-stuffed chicken breasts are smothered in a zesty tomato sauce and served atop noodles.

2 cups uncooked noodles (about 4 ounces)

2 tablespoons chopped onion

1 clove garlic, minced

1 tablespoon water

4 cups torn fresh spinach (about 4 ounces)

½ cup shredded carrot (1 medium)

1 tablespoon grated Parmesan cheese

¼ teaspoon salt

Dash pepper

4 skinned and boned chicken breasts (about 1 pound)

1 8-ounce can tomato sauce

¼ teaspoon Italian seasoning

Snipped fresh parsley

1. Cook noodles as directed on package. Drain, rinse, and set aside.

2. Combine onion, garlic, and water in 1½-quart microwave-safe casserole.

3. MICROWAVE (high), uncovered, 1½–2 minutes or until tender. Add spinach and carrots. Cover with casserole lid.

4. MICROWAVE (high) 4–5 minutes or until tender, stirring once. Add cheese, salt, and pepper; mix lightly.

5. Flatten each chicken breast by placing between plastic wrap and pounding with rolling pin until ¼-inch thick. Spoon scant ¼ cup spinach mixture onto each breast. Roll up with filling inside. Fasten with toothpick if necessary. Return to 1-quart casserole, placing seam side down. Spoon tomato sauce onto breasts; sprinkle with Italian seasoning. Cover.

6. MICROWAVE (medium-high—70%) 8–10 minutes or until chicken is done, rotating dish once. Spoon noodles onto microwave-safe serving plate. Top with chicken. Spoon sauce over all.

7. MICROWAVE (high), uncovered, 2–3 minutes or until heated through. Sprinkle with parsley.

TIPS

• A 10-ounce package frozen chopped spinach can be substituted for fresh. Microwave in package 3–4 minutes or until thawed. Drain, squeezing out excess liquid. Combine with carrot and continue as directed in step 3.

• To use full power instead of medium-high power in step 6, microwave 4 minutes, let stand 3 minutes, rotate dish, and microwave 3–4 minutes.

• Individual servings can be frozen. To reheat, microwave (medium-high—70%) 5–6 minutes.

CROWNED TURKEY WITH STUFFING BALLS

About 6 servings, 330 calories each

Sliced turkey breast, stuffing balls, acorn squash slices, and broccoli combine for a dish that looks fit for a king. The calorie count was calculated assuming that about half the turkey is used with this combination and the remainder for another meal.

1 medium acorn squash (about 1½ pounds)

½ tablespoon grated Parmesan cheese

½ tablespoon dry bread crumbs

½ teaspoon salt

½ teaspoon snipped chives

¼ teaspoon paprika

1 3-pound turkey breast, skinned

2 cups (8 ounces) sliced fresh mushrooms

1 small onion, chopped

½ cup sliced celery

2 tablespoons margarine

1½ cups dry herb-seasoned stuffing mix

1 egg, beaten

1 10-ounce package frozen chopped broccoli

¼ teaspoon seasoned salt

1. Prick squash with fork several times. Place stem side down on paper towel in microwave oven.

2. MICROWAVE (high) 8–10 minutes or until just about tender, turning squash over once if necessary. Set aside.

3. Combine Parmesan cheese, bread crumbs, salt, chives, and paprika on waxed paper. Moisten turkey breast with a little water. Roll in crumb mixture to coat evenly. Place in oven-cooking bag, set in microwave-safe baking dish. Secure opening with nylon tie. Cut six ½-inch slits in top of bag.

4. MICROWAVE (medium—50%) 30–35 minutes or until internal temperature registers 160°F. Let stand about 15 minutes.

5. Combine mushrooms, onion, celery, and 1 tablespoon of the margarine in 4-cup microwave-safe measure.

6. MICROWAVE (high), uncovered, 3–3½ minutes or until just about tender. Stir in stuffing mix and egg. Shape mixture into six balls. Set aside.

7. MICROWAVE (high) broccoli in package (remove foil overwrap if necessary) 3–4 minutes or until thawed. Drain and set aside. Cut squash in half horizontally. Scoop out seeds. Cut each half into three slices. Arrange slices around outer edge of 12-inch round microwave-safe serving plate. Top each slice with a stuffing ball. Arrange broccoli between slices. Cover with plastic wrap.

8. MICROWAVE (high) 5–6 minutes or until stuffing is set and broccoli is tender, rotating plate once. Slice turkey and arrange slices in center of plate. Combine remaining 1 tablespoon margarine and seasoned salt in small microwave-safe dish.

9. MICROWAVE (high), uncovered, 30–45 seconds or until melted. Drizzle over broccoli.

TIPS

- To use full power instead of medium power in step 4, use intervals of 5 minutes microwave and 5 minutes stand for the 30–35 minutes.

- A covered casserole or baking dish can be substituted for oven-cooking bag. Turn turkey over once during cooking time in step 4; slightly longer cooking time may be necessary in this step.

- If microwave oven does not accommodate a 12-inch round serving plate, use an oval or oblong plate that will fit inside oven.

TURKEY AND HAM ROLL-UPS

About 4 servings, 350 calories each

Rolls of turkey and ham are combined with mashed potatoes and a colorful blend of carrots and broccoli. You're sure to enjoy this attractive and tasty combination.

6 medium carrots, cut 1-inch thick (about 3 cups)

2 tablespoons water

4 medium potatoes, peeled and quartered (about 1 pound)

¼ cup water

½ teaspoon salt

Dash white pepper

½–¾ cup skim milk

4 turkey cutlets (about 12 ounces)

4 slices boiled ham

1 ounce Swiss or mozzarella cheese

⅛ teaspoon nutmeg

2 tablespoons dry bread crumbs

1 tablespoon grated Parmesan cheese

1 teaspoon parsley flakes

¼ teaspoon paprika

2 cups fresh broccoli pieces

1 tablespoon margarine

1 teaspoon grated fresh orange peel

1. Combine carrots and 2 tablespoons water in 4-cup microwave-safe measure. Cover with plastic wrap. Combine potatoes and ¼ cup water in 1-quart microwave-safe casserole. Cover with casserole lid. Place containers side-by-side in microwave oven.

2. MICROWAVE (high) 12–14 minutes or until potatoes and carrots are tender, stirring each once. Drain carrots and set aside. Drain potatoes. Mash with potato masher or mixer. Add salt and pepper. Beat in milk until light and fluffy. Set aside.

3. Place cutlets between plastic wrap and pound with rolling pin until ¼ inch thick. Place a ham slice on each cutlet. Cut cheese into 4 sticks; place in center of cutlets. Sprinkle with nutmeg. Roll up with cheese inside. If necessary, fasten with toothpicks. Combine bread crumbs, Parmesan cheese, parsley, and paprika; mix well. Coat each turkey roll with crumbs. Place in 12-by 8-inch microwave-safe baking dish. Cover with waxed paper.

4. MICROWAVE (medium-high—70%) 6–8 minutes or until turkey is just about done, rotating dish once. Move rolls to outside of dish. Spoon mashed potatoes down center of dish. Place turkey rolls on potatoes. Arrange carrots and broccoli around potatoes. Cover with plastic wrap.

5. MICROWAVE (high) 4–5 minutes or until broccoli is tender, rotating dish once. Set aside.

6. MICROWAVE (high) margarine in uncovered small microwave-safe dish 30–60 seconds or until melted. Spoon over potatoes. Sprinkle carrots and broccoli with orange peel.

TIPS

- To use full power instead of medium-high power in step 4, microwave 4–6 minutes, rotating dish twice.

- To help keep cheese inside of rolls, enclose it in the ham before rolling up inside of turkey cutlets.

- Skinned and boned chicken breast can be substituted for turkey.

ELEGANT FISH ROLLS

**About 4 servings,
340 calories each**

Salmon-stuffed sole fillets are surrounded by new potatoes and fresh asparagus in this delectable meal.

1 pound new potatoes

¼ cup water

1 pound fresh asparagus spears, trimmed

2 tablespoons margarine

¼ teaspoon dill weed

¼ cup chopped celery

2 green onions, sliced (including tops)

1 6½-ounce can salmon, drained

1 egg, beaten

2 tablespoons reduced-calorie sour cream

1 tablespoon dry white wine (optional)

¼ teaspoon thyme leaves

1 pound sole fillets

1 tablespoon snipped fresh parsley

1. Scrub potatoes and cut a thin strip of peel from center of each. Place potatoes and water in 1½-quart microwave-safe casserole. Cover with casserole lid.

2. MICROWAVE (high) 7–8 minutes or until just about tender, stirring once. Add asparagus spears. Cover.

3. MICROWAVE (high) 4–5 minutes or until tender. Drain; add 1 tablespoon of the margarine and dill weed. Set aside partially covered.

4. MICROWAVE (high) celery and onions in uncovered microwave-safe dish 1–1½ minutes or until tender. Remove large bones from salmon; flake apart and add to onion mixture. Mix in egg, sour cream, wine, and thyme. Divide mixture among sole fillets. Roll up with salmon mixture inside. Place seam side down in 12- by 8-inch microwave-safe baking dish. Cut remaining 1 tablespoon margarine into 4 pieces and place a piece on each fish roll. Cover with plastic wrap.

5. MICROWAVE (high) 5–6 minutes or until fish flakes apart easily with fork, rotating dish once. Arrange asparagus spears and potatoes around fish. Spoon butter mixture from fish over vegetables.

6. MICROWAVE (high) 2–3 minutes or until heated through. Sprinkle fish with parsley.

TIPS

● About 4 ounces cooked fresh salmon can be substituted for canned. Add ¼ teaspoon salt if unsalted.

● An 8-ounce package frozen asparagus spears can be substituted for fresh.

● Plain yogurt can be substituted for sour cream.

HERBED SALMON STEAKS WITH RICE

About 4 servings, 350 calories each

Colorful vegetables add a special touch to the rice complementing these flavorful salmon steaks. Serve with a tossed salad and you have a very special meal.

1 cup chopped celery

1 cup (4 ounces) sliced fresh mushrooms

½ cup chopped green pepper

1 small onion, chopped

⅔ cup uncooked long-grain rice

1 cup water

1 teaspoon instant chicken bouillon

1 teaspoon parsley flakes

1 10-ounce package frozen peas and carrots

1 teaspoon seasoned salt

1 teaspoon tarragon leaves

½ teaspoon marjoram leaves

¼ teaspoon garlic powder

4 salmon steaks, cut ½-inch thick (about 1 pound)

4 lemon slices (optional)

1. Combine celery, mushrooms, green pepper, and onion in 2-quart microwave-safe casserole. Cover with casserole lid.

2. MICROWAVE (high) 3–4 minutes or until just about tender. Stir in rice, water, bouillon, and parsley. Cover.

3. MICROWAVE (high) 7–8 minutes or until mixture boils. Add frozen peas and carrots. Cover.

4. MICROWAVE (high) 7–8 minutes or until most of liquid is absorbed. Set aside covered. Combine seasoned salt, tarragon, marjoram, and garlic powder. Sprinkle both sides of salmon steaks with mixture. Place steaks on shallow microwave-safe plate or baking dish. Cover with plastic wrap.

5. MICROWAVE (high) 4–4½ minutes or until fish flakes apart easily with fork. Spoon rice around salmon steaks.

6. MICROWAVE (high), uncovered, 2–3 minutes or until rice is heated through. Garnish salmon with lemon slices, if desired.

GARLIC SHRIMP AND VEGETABLE MEDLEY

**About 6 servings,
200 calories each**

This entree of shrimp and vegetables is special enough for company, yet simple enough for a family meal.

3 medium potatoes, peeled (about 1 pound)

3 medium carrots, sliced (about 2 cups)

1 9-ounce package frozen French-cut green beans

3 tablespoons margarine

3 green onions, sliced (including tops)

1–2 cloves garlic, minced

2 tablespoons dry white wine

1½ pounds medium-size fresh or frozen uncooked shrimp, thawed

Dash hot pepper sauce

1. Cut potatoes into matchstick pieces, about 2 inches long. Rinse well in cold water; drain. Arrange on one side of 12-inch round microwave-safe serving plate. Place carrots on other side of plate. Unwrap green beans and place next to carrots. Cover with plastic wrap.

2. MICROWAVE (high) 12–14 minutes or until tender-crisp, rotating plate once. Lift one corner of wrap and drain juices. Let stand partially covered.

3. Combine margarine, onions, and garlic in 1-quart microwave-safe casserole.

4. MICROWAVE (high), uncovered, 1½–2 minutes or until tender. Stir in wine, shrimp, and pepper sauce. Cover with casserole lid.

5. MICROWAVE (high) 5–6 minutes or until shrimp are pink and firm, stirring once. Separate potatoes and green beans by pushing them toward carrots. Spoon shrimp into open area on plate. Spoon cooking juices from shrimp over vegetables and shrimp.

6. MICROWAVE (high), uncovered, 2–3 minutes or until heated through.

TIPS

- An 8-ounce package frozen asparagus spears can be substituted for green beans.

- If microwave oven does not accommodate a 12-inch round serving plate, use an oval or oblong plate that will fit inside oven.

CAJUN SHRIMP

**About 4 servings,
265 calories each**

Enjoy this spicy blend of shrimp and vegetables on a bed of fettuccini. A roll and gelatin salad would complete this meal nicely.

4 ounces uncooked fettuccini, broken into thirds

1 large onion, sliced

1 cup sliced celery

2 cloves garlic, minced

2 tablespoons water

2 cups sliced fresh cauliflower pieces

3 medium zucchini, cut ½ inch thick (2 cups)

1 cup fresh broccoli pieces

1 cup (4 ounces) sliced fresh mushrooms

2 cups skim milk

3 tablespoons flour

½ teaspoon salt

½ teaspoon paprika

½ teaspoon thyme leaves

⅛ teaspoon pepper

4–6 drops hot pepper sauce

12 ounces medium-size fresh or frozen uncooked shrimp, thawed

1. Cook fettuccini as directed on package. Drain, rinse, and set aside.

2. Combine onion, celery, garlic, and water in 2-quart microwave-safe casserole.

3. MICROWAVE (high), uncovered, 2–2½ minutes or until just about tender. Add cauliflower, zucchini, broccoli, and mushrooms. Cover with casserole lid.

4. MICROWAVE (high) 7–8 minutes or until tender-crisp, stirring once. Drain juices into 4-cup microwave-safe measure. Let vegetables stand uncovered. Add milk and flour to measure; mix until smooth. Stir in salt, paprika, thyme, pepper, pepper sauce, and shrimp.

5. MICROWAVE (high), uncovered, 6–8 minutes or until mixture boils and thickens and shrimp are pink and firm, stirring twice. Pour over vegetables; mix lightly.

6. Arrange fettuccini on large microwave-safe serving plate. Spoon vegetable mixture over fettuccini.

7. MICROWAVE (high), uncovered, 2–3 minutes or until heated through.

SKEWERED SHRIMP ON RICE PILAF

**About 4 servings,
200 calories each**

Marinated shrimp kabobs cook atop a flavorful bed of rice. Serve with crusty bread and a plate of tropical fruit.

¼ cup lemon juice

2 green onions, sliced (including tops)

1 clove garlic, minced

1 tablespoon honey

¼ teaspoon tarragon leaves

8 ounces medium-size fresh or frozen uncooked shrimp, thawed

1 cup hot water

½ cup shredded carrot (about 1 medium)

¼ cup snipped fresh parsley

1 tablespoon margarine

¼ teaspoon salt

1 cup quick-cooking rice

1 green pepper, cut into 12 pieces

8 cherry tomatoes

4 10-inch wooden skewers

1. Combine lemon juice, green onions, garlic, honey, and tarragon in bowl or plastic bag. Add shrimp and mix lightly to coat evenly. Let stand at room temperature about 30 minutes to marinate.

2. Combine water, carrot, parsley, margarine, and salt in 10- by 6-inch microwave-safe baking dish. Cover with plastic wrap.

3. MICROWAVE (high) 4–5 minutes or until carrot is tender and water is steaming. Mix in rice with fork. Alternate shrimp, green pepper, and cherry tomatoes on wooden skewers. Lay across dish. Brush shrimp with additional marinade. Cover with waxed paper.

4. MICROWAVE (high) 3–4 minutes or until shrimp are pink and firm, rotating dish once. Brush with marinade again before serving.

CRAB ALFREDO

**About 6 servings,
270 calories each**

A delicate flavor and touch of elegance make this combination perfect for a special dinner or luncheon. Serve it on one large plate or in individual dishes or shells.

6 ounces uncooked linguine

2 cups (8 ounces) sliced fresh mushrooms

1 small onion, chopped

1 tablespoon margarine

1 tablespoon flour

1 cup evaporated skim milk

¼ teaspoon basil leaves

¼ teaspoon garlic salt

⅛ teaspoon oregano leaves

Dash pepper

2 tablespoons dry sherry (optional)

1 10-ounce package frozen chopped spinach

2 tablespoons grated Parmesan cheese

12 ounces cooked crabmeat, flaked

2 tablespoons lemon juice

1. Cook linguine as directed on package. Drain, rinse, and set aside.

2. Combine mushrooms, onion, and margarine in 1-quart microwave-safe casserole.

3. MICROWAVE (high), uncovered, 3–4 minutes or until just about tender. Stir in flour, milk, basil, garlic salt, oregano, and pepper.

4. MICROWAVE (high), uncovered, 4–5 minutes or until mixture boils and thickens, stirring once. Stir in sherry.

5. MICROWAVE (high) spinach in package (remove foil overwrap if necessary) 3–4 minutes or until thawed. Drain, squeezing out excess moisture.

6. Spread linguine in bottom of 10-inch round microwave-safe baking dish. Add sauce and mix lightly. Spoon spinach over linguine; sprinkle with Parmesan cheese. Mix crabmeat with lemon juice; sprinkle over cheese. Cover with plastic wrap.

7. MICROWAVE (high) 3–4 minutes or until heated through (150°F), rotating dish once.

SCALLOPS AND BROCCOLI TETRAZZINI

About 4 servings, 325 calories each

This quick and appealing seafood entree is ideal for a small gathering. For a less expensive meal, substitute cod or torsk chunks for part or all of the scallops.

4 ounces uncooked vermicelli

2 green onions, sliced (including tops)

2 tablespoons chopped green pepper

2 tablespoons chopped celery

1 clove garlic, minced

1 tablespoon margarine

2 tablespoons flour

2 teaspoons instant chicken bouillon

1/4 teaspoon dill weed

1/8 teaspoon hot pepper sauce

1 cup skim milk

3 tablespoons dry white wine

12 ounces fresh or frozen scallops, thawed

1 egg, beaten

3 cups fresh broccoli pieces

1/4 teaspoon tarragon leaves

Lemon wedges

1. Cook vermicelli as directed on package. Drain, rinse, and set aside.

2. Combine onions, green pepper, celery, garlic, and margarine in 1½-quart microwave-safe casserole.

3. MICROWAVE (high), uncovered, 1½–2 minutes or until just about tender. Stir in flour, bouillon, dill weed, pepper sauce, milk, and wine until smooth.

4. MICROWAVE (high), uncovered, 3–4 minutes or until mixture boils and thickens, stirring once. Cut scallops into ½-inch pieces if necessary. Stir scallops and egg into sauce, mixing well.

5. MICROWAVE (medium-high—70%), uncovered, 3–4 minutes or until scallops are set and tender, stirring once. Set aside.

6. MICROWAVE (high) broccoli in covered 4-cup microwave-safe measure 3–4 minutes or until just about tender. Stir in tarragon. Place vermicelli in center of microwave-safe serving plate. Spoon scallop mixture over vermicelli. Arrange broccoli around edge of plate.

7. MICROWAVE (high), uncovered, 4–5 minutes or until heated through, rotating plate once. Serve with lemon wedges.

TIPS

- If desired, assemble in individual casseroles or shells.

- To use full power instead of medium-high power in step 5, reduce time to 2½–3½ minutes, stirring twice.

LEG OF LAMB DINNER

**About 8 servings,
350 calories each**

Lamb microwaves moist and tender. New potatoes, peas, and carrots add a touch of spring to the finished dish.

1 4-pound leg of lamb roast

2 cloves garlic, quartered

8 1-inch strips lemon peel

1 teaspoon browning and
   seasoning sauce

2 teaspoons water

1 teaspoon marjoram leaves

16 new potatoes (about 1¾
   pounds)

2 cups sliced carrots (about 4
   medium)

½ cup water

1 10-ounce package frozen peas

1 tablespoon margarine

1 tablespoon snipped fresh
   mint

½ teaspoon salt

1 tablespoon lemon juice

Salt and pepper (optional)

1. Trim excess fat from roast. Place fat side up on microwave-safe roasting rack. Make slits about ¼ inch into fat layer and meat; insert garlic and lemon peel. Mix together seasoning sauce and 2 teaspoons water; brush over roast. Sprinkle with marjoram. Cover with waxed paper.

2. MICROWAVE (medium—50%) 40–45 minutes or until internal temperature registers 150° F, turning meat over once. Cover and let stand.

3. Scrub potatoes and cut a thin strip of peel from center of each or peel the potatoes. Combine with carrots and ½ cup water in 2-quart microwave-safe casserole. Cover with casserole lid.

4. MICROWAVE (high) 10–12 minutes or until just about tender, stirring once. Add peas. Cover.

5. MICROWAVE (high) 4–5 minutes or until tender. Drain. Add margarine, mint, salt, and lemon juice; stir to coat vegetables with mixture.

6. Slice lamb and place in center of microwave-safe serving plate. Arrange vegetables around lamb. Season lamb with salt and pepper if desired.

TIPS

● When in season, use 2 cups shelled fresh peas.

● Natural meat browning and seasoning powder can be sprinkled over roast rather than brushing with seasoning sauce mixture.

● To substitute dry mint for fresh, use about ¼ teaspoon.

● To use full power instead of medium power in step 2, use intervals of 5 minutes microwave and 5 minutes stand for the 40–45 minutes.

ROAST BEEF AND VEGETABLES

About 6 servings, 340 calories each

Roast beef, potatoes, and vegetables combine on one attractive platter. While the meat stands after cooking, the vegetables microwave to perfection.

3 medium baking potatoes, scrubbed

2 pounds eye of round beef roast

1 tablespoon Dijon-style mustard

1 teaspoon Worcestershire sauce

½ teaspoon garlic salt

½ teaspoon basil leaves

2 cups fresh cauliflower pieces

2 cups sliced carrots (about 4 medium)

2 tablespoons water

2 cups (8 ounces) sliced fresh mushrooms

Water

1 tablespoon cornstarch

1 teaspoon instant beef bouillon

⅛ teaspoon pepper

Nutmeg

Fresh parsley sprigs

1. Prick potatoes several times with fork. Place on paper towel in microwave oven.

2. MICROWAVE (high) 10–12 minutes or until just about tender, turning potatoes over once. Set aside.

3. Place roast in 12- by 8-inch microwave-safe baking dish. Combine mustard, Worcestershire sauce, garlic salt, and basil; mix well. Spread over meat. Cover with waxed paper.

4. MICROWAVE (high) 5 minutes. Then, MICROWAVE (medium—50%) 15–18 minutes or until internal temperature registers 140°F, turning meat over halfway through cooking time. Let stand covered.

5. Combine cauliflower, carrots, and 2 tablespoons water in 1-quart microwave-safe casserole. Cover with casserole lid.

6. MICROWAVE (high) 8–10 minutes or until tender, stirring once. Set aside covered. Place mushrooms in 4-cup microwave-safe measure. Cover with plastic wrap.

7. MICROWAVE (high) 2½–3 minutes or until tender. Drain drippings from meat and add water to make 1 cup. Add mushrooms. Blend in cornstarch, bouillon, and pepper.

8. MICROWAVE (high), uncovered, 1½–2 minutes or until mixture boils and thickens, stirring once. Slice meat and arrange in center of baking dish. If desired, spoon some of mushroom sauce over meat. Cut potatoes in half and arrange along one side of dish; spoon cauliflower and carrots into other side of dish; sprinkle nutmeg over vegetables.

9. MICROWAVE (high), uncovered, 4–5 minutes or until heated through. Garnish with parsley. Serve with remaining mushroom sauce.

TIPS

- Other vegetable combinations can be substituted for carrots and cauliflower.

- The calorie count was calculated assuming that one-fourth of the roast is left for another meal.

BEEF AND RICE NOODLES TERIYAKI

**About 6 servings,
280 calories each**

Marinated steaks are browned and served with an appealing combination of Oriental noodles and vegetables. For best flavor and tenderness allow meat to marinate overnight.

1 pound beef round or tip steak, cut ½-inch thick

3 green onions, sliced (including tops)

1 clove garlic, minced

¼ cup soy sauce

2 tablespoons brown sugar

3 tablespoons dry sherry

1 teaspoon sesame seed

2 teaspoons cooking oil

⅛ teaspoon ground ginger

5 cups hot water

1 7-ounce package Oriental-style noodles (rice noodles)

1 16-ounce package frozen Japanese-style vegetables

1 6-ounce package frozen pea pods

1 teaspoon cornstarch

1. Pound meat with meat mallet or side of saucer to help tenderize. Place in 10- by 6-inch glass dish. Combine onions, garlic, soy sauce, brown sugar, sherry, sesame seed, 1 teaspoon of the oil, and ginger; mix well. Pour over meat. Turn meat to coat evenly. Cover with plastic wrap. Refrigerate overnight, turning meat once to keep coated with marinade.

2. MICROWAVE (high) water in uncovered 2-quart microwave-safe mixing bowl 7–8 minutes or until boiling. Break noodles in half and add to boiling water.

3. MICROWAVE (high), uncovered, 2–3 minutes or until noodles are just about tender. Drain. Add frozen vegetables. Cover with plastic wrap.

4. MICROWAVE (high) 8–9 minutes or until vegetables are just about tender. Drain, add pea pods, and set aside partially covered.

5. MICROWAVE (high) microwave browning dish 6–8 minutes or as directed for meats by manufacturer. Coat dish lightly with remaining 1 teaspoon oil. Remove steaks from marinade; remove excess marinade with paper towel. Place steaks on hot dish.

6. MICROWAVE (high), uncovered, 1 minute. Turn steaks over.

7. MICROWAVE (high), uncovered, 30–60 seconds or until cooked to desired doneness. Transfer marinade to 2-cup microwave-safe measure; drain cooking juices from meat into measure. Stir in cornstarch.

8. MICROWAVE (high), uncovered, 1–1½ minutes or until mixture boils and thickens, stirring once. Mix with noodles and vegetables. Arrange on large microwave-safe serving plate. Top with steaks.

9. MICROWAVE (high), uncovered, 2–3 minutes or until heated through.

TIPS

● To substitute fresh ginger root, use ½ teaspoon grated.

● If a microwave browning dish is not available, brown steaks in a little oil in frying pan over medium-high heat on range.

COMPANY PORK ROAST

**About 6 servings,
345 calories each**

*Tender pork slices and crumb-coated potato fans surround gingered carrots and pea
pods. The calories in this combination were calculated assuming that ½ pound of the
roast is left over for another meal.*

**6 small potatoes, peeled (about
2 pounds)**

**2 pounds boneless lean pork
roast**

Garlic salt

Pepper

1½ tablespoons margarine

1 tablespoon cornflake crumbs

**1 tablespoon grated Parmesan
cheese**

¼ teaspoon seasoned salt

**4 medium carrots, cut 1 inch
thick (2 cups)**

**1 6-ounce package frozen pea
pods**

1 teaspoon sesame seed

⅛ teaspoon ground ginger

Fresh parsley sprigs (optional)

1. Cut about six ¼-inch slices ⅔ of the way through
each potato. Soak in ice water. Sprinkle roast
with garlic salt and pepper. Place in oven-
cooking bag, set in microwave-safe baking dish.
Secure opening with nylon tie. Cut six ½-inch
slits in top of bag.

2. MICROWAVE (medium—50%) 22–25 minutes or
until internal temperature registers 160°F. Let
stand covered. Drain and remove excess
moisture from potatoes with paper towels.

3. MICROWAVE (high) 1 tablespoon of the
margarine in uncovered microwave-safe dish
30–45 seconds or until melted. Combine
cornflake crumbs, Parmesan cheese, and
seasoned salt. Brush each potato with margarine;
then coat with crumb mixture. Place cut side up
spoke-fashion around outer edge of 12-inch
round microwave-safe serving plate. Place
carrots in center of plate. Cover with plastic
wrap.

4. MICROWAVE (high) 10–11 minutes or until
potatoes are just about tender, rotating plate
once. Break apart frozen pea pods and place on
carrots. Cover.

5. MICROWAVE (high) 10–11 minutes or until
potatoes are tender. Slice meat and arrange
among potatoes on plate. Combine remaining
½ tablespoon margarine, sesame seed, and ginger
in small microwave-safe dish.

6. MICROWAVE (high) 30–45 seconds or until
melted. Drizzle over pea pods and carrots; mix
lightly. Garnish pork with parsley.

7. MICROWAVE (high), uncovered, 2–3 minutes or
until heated through.

TIPS

- If using larger potatoes, cut each in half crosswise. Then make lengthwise slices in potato halves.

- Two cups fresh pea pods or snap peas can be substituted for frozen.

- If microwave oven does not accommodate a 12-inch round serving plate, use an oval or oblong plate that will fit inside oven.

- Full power is not recommended for pork roasts.

STUFFED PORK TENDERLOIN ROLLS

**About 6 servings,
205 calories each**

A savory blend of herb stuffing flavors pork rolls while a combination of cheesy cauliflower and broccoli add color to the final presentation.

3 tablespoons chopped onion

3 tablespoons chopped green pepper

2 tablespoons sesame seed

1 tablespoon margarine

1½ cups dry herb-seasoned stuffing mix

1 teaspoon Worcestershire sauce

1 teaspoon lemon juice

1 egg, slightly beaten

1 pound pork tenderloin, cut into 6 pieces

1 tablespoon cooking oil

½ teaspoon paprika

1 medium head cauliflower

1 pound trimmed fresh broccoli

¼ cup shredded cheddar cheese

Seasoned salt

1. Combine onion, green pepper, sesame seed, and margarine in 4-cup microwave-safe measure.

2. MICROWAVE (high), uncovered, 2½–3 minutes or until just about tender. Stir in stuffing mix, Worcestershire sauce, lemon juice, and egg. Flatten tenderloin if necessary, by placing between plastic wrap and pounding with rolling pin until ¼ inch thick. Divide stuffing mixture among pork pieces. Roll up with stuffing inside; if necessary, fasten with toothpicks.

3. Heat oil in skillet over medium-high heat on range. Add pork rolls, sprinkle with paprika, and brown on all sides. Set aside.

4. Cut a cone-shaped piece from core of cauliflower to help center cook more quickly. Place stem side down on large microwave-safe serving plate. Cover with plastic wrap.

5. MICROWAVE (high) 6–7 minutes or until heated through. Arrange pork rolls around cauliflower. Cut broccoli into pieces with stems no more than ¼ inch thick. Arrange broccoli between pork rolls. Cover with plastic wrap.

6. MICROWAVE (high) 5–6 minutes or until broccoli and pork are cooked, rotating plate once. Sprinkle broccoli and cauliflower with cheese and seasoned salt. Let stand a few minutes to melt cheese.

TIP

• Already cut and flattened tenderloin patties can be used.

PEACHY PORK TENDERLOIN PLATTER

About 8 servings, 350 calories each

Juicy pork tenderloin is topped with a tasty peach sauce and surrounded with poppy seed noodles and green beans.

3 cups uncooked noodles (6 ounces)

1 16-ounce can sliced peaches in own juice

Water

1 tablespoon cornstarch

1 teaspoon brown sugar

½ teaspoon grated fresh ginger root

1 teaspoon lemon juice

2 whole pork tenderloins (2 pounds)

Natural meat browning and seasoning powder

2 9-ounce packages frozen French-cut green beans

2 tablespoons margarine

1 8-ounce can sliced water chestnuts, drained

½ teaspoon summer savory

1. Cook noodles as directed on package. Drain, rinse, and set aside.

2. Drain liquid from peaches into 2-cup microwave-safe measure. Add water to make ¾ cup. Stir in cornstarch, brown sugar, ginger root, and lemon juice.

3. MICROWAVE (high), uncovered, 1½–2 minutes or until mixture boils and thickens, stirring once. Set aside. Arrange tenderloins in 12- by 8-inch microwave-safe baking dish, leaving about 1 inch of space between tenderloins. Sprinkle all sides with browning powder. Cover with waxed paper.

4. MICROWAVE (high) 10–12 minutes or until pork is done (160°F), turning tenderloins over once. Drain drippings into peach sauce. Cover pork and let stand 10–15 minutes.

5. MICROWAVE (high) beans in packages (remove foil overwrap if necessary) 9–11 minutes or until heated through, turning packages over once.

6. MICROWAVE (high) margarine in uncovered small microwave-safe dish 30–60 seconds or until melted. Arrange noodles in center of large microwave-safe serving plate. Slice pork and arrange on noodles. Place beans on either side of noodles. Top beans with water chestnuts, mixing lightly. Add savory to margarine; drizzle over beans. Spoon peach sauce over pork and noodles. Garnish plate with peach slices.

7. MICROWAVE (high) 3–5 minutes or until heated through, rotating plate once.

TIPS

● If desired, omit browning powder and brush pork with a mixture of 1 tablespoon soy sauce and ¼ teaspoon paprika.

● To substitute ground ginger for fresh, use ⅛ teaspoon.

VEAL LOUISA

**About 6 servings,
325 calories each**

Cubes of veal are simmered in a flavorful stroganoff sauce, then served over a blend of white and wild rice. Tomato halves add a pretty color.

¼ cup wild rice

1¾ cups water

⅔ cup uncooked long-grain white rice

½ teaspoon salt

1 tablespoon margarine

1 pound cubed boneless veal

1 tablespoon flour

1 medium onion, chopped

1 clove garlic, minced

2 cups (8 ounces) sliced fresh mushrooms

½ cup water

¼ cup dry white wine or water

1 teaspoon instant beef bouillon

½ teaspoon thyme leaves

¼ teaspoon summer savory

¼ cup reduced-calorie sour cream

1 tablespoon snipped fresh parsley

3 medium tomatoes, cored

Salt

⅛ teaspoon basil leaves

1 tablespoon grated Parmesan cheese

1. Combine wild rice and ¾ cup of the water in 1½-quart microwave-safe casserole. Cover with casserole lid.

2. MICROWAVE (high) 2½–3 minutes or until mixture boils. Let stand covered 1–2 hours.

3. MICROWAVE (high) rice mixture 3–4 minutes or until boiling. Let stand 10 minutes. Add remaining 1 cup water, white rice, and ½ teaspoon salt. Cover.

4. MICROWAVE (high) 5–6 minutes or until mixture boils. Then, MICROWAVE (medium—50%) 14–16 minutes or until rice is tender and liquid is absorbed. Uncover and set aside.

5. Heat margarine in shallow 1½-quart pyroceramic casserole over medium-high heat on range. Coat veal with flour; brown in margarine on all sides. Add onion and garlic; continue cooking until lightly browned. Stir in any remaining flour, mushrooms, water, wine, bouillon, thyme, and savory. Cover with casserole lid.

6. MICROWAVE (medium-high—70%) 12–14 minutes or until veal is tender and flavors are blended, stirring once. Stir in sour cream.

7. Fluff rice with fork; spoon into center of large microwave-safe serving plate, making slight indentation in center. Spoon veal mixture onto rice. Sprinkle with parsley. Cut each tomato in half crosswise. Place cut side up around rice mixture. Sprinkle with salt, basil, and Parmesan cheese.

8. MICROWAVE (high), uncovered, 3–5 minutes or until tomatoes are heated, rotating plate once.

TIPS

- To use full power instead of medium power in step 4, use periods of 5 minutes microwave and 3 minutes stand for the 14–16 minutes. In step 6, microwave 5 minutes, let stand 5 minutes and then microwave 3–5 minutes, stirring several times.

- Cubed lean pork can be substituted for veal; or, try with boneless chicken or turkey.

- Plain yogurt can be substituted for sour cream.

CHAPTER
6
FREEZER DISHES

Today's lifestyles find more and more people eating alone or fixing and eating meals on the run. In the process we often rely on less nutritional foods. With a microwave oven and freezer, you can team your resources and have well-balanced nutritious meals in just minutes.

Rather than include a chapter of freezer dishes that often require longer to heat than the initial preparation time, we have included timings throughout the book for those foods that freeze well. The emphasis is on individual servings since this is the size that heats the easiest and quickest in the microwave. It is the kind of food that fits the need for a quick meal on the run. Since the recipes in this book usually include a protein, vegetable, and starch, the combinations make good single-serving meals. If you want extras, add some fruit, a salad, and/or a roll.

On the pages that follow are basic freezing tips for preparing the foods as well as the guidelines for heating. Individual timings are given with many recipes in the "Tips" throughout the book. Whether you plan to have extras to freeze in individual servings or you just plate the leftovers and freeze, you can have a wealth of table-ready foods waiting for you in the freezer. Dinner on the run may be something we have to live with at various times, but it need not mean a lot of last minute hassle and poor eating habits.

FREEZING INDIVIDUAL SERVINGS FOR LATER REHEATING

Here are guidelines and tips to follow to assure optimum quality and results from your own homemade freezer meals.

WHY INDIVIDUAL SERVINGS? Smaller quantities reheat more quickly and with less chance of overcooking the outside edges. Often we only need one or two servings of a food from the freezer. Frequently, it is quicker to cook a one-dish meal for four people than it is to thaw and heat the same meal that is ready in the freezer.

HOW IMPORTANT IS ARRANGEMENT? When the dish includes several different types of food, it is best to place the thicker, more dense items near the edge and the lighter-textured, smaller pieces in the center. When possible, keep the food in the very center of the dish as thin as possible. This way it will take much less time to heat the center. This technique is helpful even with the easier-to-heat foods that can be stirred.

WHAT DISHES TO USE? Use a container that will adequately hold the contents without a lot of extra air space. There are many individual glass and plastic dishes and serving plates that are ideal. Some containers come with covers for freezer use, while others need to be sealed inside a freezer bag or wrapped tightly in foil. If you purchase commercially frozen foods for reheating in the microwave, you can often get several more uses from these dishes. When you are short on dishes, line the dish with plastic wrap and place the food in the dish until frozen. Once frozen, remove the plastic-wrapped food and package in a freezer bag. When ready to reheat, just remove the plastic wrap and return the food to the original dish.

Always be sure the wrap fits the dish tightly. Air causes food to deteriorate more rapidly, so it is best to eliminate as much air as possible from inside the container.

BE SURE TO LABEL AND DATE EACH PACKAGE! Keep freezer tape and a marker close to the freezer and be sure to label each package. You may think you will remember the contents and date you froze the package, but chances are you will wonder in a few weeks just what is in that package. Include the contents, date frozen, and either reheating time or cookbook page reference for the timings.

HOW LONG TO STORE? Most individual servings will be excellent for one month and still quite good after two months. Longer storage means lower quality of food. Keep a record on the freezer door of the various items frozen and then try to mark them off as used. It is also good to rotate items so that new ones are placed at the back, moving the older items up to the front of the freezer.

HOW LONG TO HEAT? Items that can be stirred and that are not sensitive to overheating are usually heated on high or full power. Those foods that cannot be stirred are usually better if a slightly lower power is used. If your oven has only one power level, just turn the oven off for a few minutes about halfway through the cooking time. This allows the heat to equalize without overcooking the edges. For individual servings, about 5 to 6 minutes is required when heated on high, and about 6 to 8 minutes when the food is heated on medium-high (70% power).

SHOULD FOODS BE COVERED? A covering will help the food heat more quickly. If the food is heated in a container with a microwaveable cover, you can just loosen the cover slightly and use it. Otherwise, cover with waxed paper. If the food has a crumb coating or requires some drying, use a paper towel covering. For moist, casserole-like foods, you will have best results from a tight covering such as a casserole lid or plastic wrap.

ARE ANY ADDITIONS NECESSARY BEFORE REHEATING? Sauces and pasta type products usually become thicker in consistency when stored either in the refrigerator or freezer. Adding one to two tablespoons of water before reheating will make the heated product consistency very similar to the original.

HOW CAN I TELL WHEN THE FOOD IS HOT? One of the best methods is to feel the center bottom of the container. If it still feels a little cool, the center of the food is still cool. When the center bottom feels warm, the contents should be hot enough to serve. If using a probe, set it at 140°–150°F. Of course, the probe usually cannot be inserted into the frozen food, but can be added after thawing starts. Food directly surrounding the probe often heats faster than the remainder of the dish so be sure and insert the probe in another area to test if it has also been heated. Checking the warmth of the container bottom is often the easiest way to tell if the contents are hot enough to serve.

IS A STANDING TIME NECESSARY? With foods that are stirred, very little if any standing time is needed. Layered items and other foods that cannot be stirred should be allowed to stand about five minutes before serving. This allows the heat at the edges of the food to move into the center, equalizing the temperature. After standing time, if the food still seems a little cool on the bottom, just microwave about a minute or two longer and it should be ready to serve.

CHAPTER
7
QUICK AND EASY

Many days, our schedules do not allow much time for meal preparation. The following recipes have been designed with just these busy days in mind. Each recipe uses a minimum of ingredients and can be table-ready in about twenty minutes.

The ingredients are commonly found on most kitchen shelves. To save time, prepared sauces, soups, and frozen prepared vegetables are often used. If some of these are not staples on your food shelves, you can easily make your own ingredients and choose to use fresh vegetables with little change in cooking time. Of course, the preparation may take a little longer since there would be more chopping and measuring involved.

To save time, don't rely on the microwave for all of the cooking. Use the microwave oven when it is most efficient but use the conventional range for heating large quantities of water, to cook pastas, and for foods that require longer simmering, such as rice.

So, when time is at a premium but you still want to serve a nutritious and tasty meal, look to this chapter. You will be pleasantly surprised at the lite, satisfying food you can prepare in a short amount of time.

CHICKEN STRIPS WITH ORANGE RICE

**About 4 servings,
265 calories each**

Orange juice concentrate enhances the flavor of this rice and chicken combination.

  1 tablespoon margarine
12 ounces skinned and boned chicken breast

Garlic salt

  1 cup quick-cooking rice
  1 cup hot water
  2 cups frozen vegetable combination (broccoli, cauliflower, and carrots)
  ¼ teaspoon ground ginger
  1 tablespoon frozen orange juice concentrate

1. MICROWAVE (high) margarine in uncovered 10- by 6-inch microwave-safe baking dish 30–60 seconds or until melted. Cut chicken into strips. Add to margarine, turning to coat evenly. Sprinkle with garlic salt.

2. MICROWAVE (high), uncovered, 4–5 minutes or until chicken is no longer pink, stirring once. Add rice, water, vegetables, and ginger; mix lightly. Cover with plastic wrap.

3. MICROWAVE (high) 8–10 minutes or until rice is tender. Stir in concentrate.

AZTECA SOUP

**About 5 servings,
150 calories each**

This spicy hot Mexican chicken soup will surely warm you all over. See the recipe Tips if you prefer a milder flavor.

1 small onion, chopped

1 clove garlic, minced

1 cup finely chopped carrots (about 2 medium)

2 cups water

1 14½-ounce can chicken broth

1 10-ounce can tomatoes with green chilies, undrained

8 ounces skinned and boned chicken breast, cut into thin strips

4 corn tortillas (about 6-inch size)

1. Combine onion, garlic, carrots, and ½ cup of the water in 2-quart microwave-safe casserole. Cover with casserole lid.

2. MICROWAVE (high) 5–6 minutes or until vegetables are tender. Add remaining 1½ cups water, chicken broth, tomatoes, and chicken. Cover.

3. MICROWAVE (high) 8–10 minutes or until chicken is done and mixture is hot, stirring twice. Cut tortillas in half and then into ½-inch strips. Add to soup. Let stand a few minutes before serving.

TIPS

- For a milder soup, use a 16-ounce can of tomatoes, undrained and cut into small pieces, instead of the tomatoes with chilies. Reduce water to 1 cup. Add 2 to 4 tablespoons chopped mild green chilies and ¾ teaspoon salt.

- Leftover cooked chicken can be substituted for fresh. Use about 2 cups cubed chicken.

CHICKEN-POTATO BAKE

**About 4 servings,
280 calories each**

*Frozen hash browns, vegetables, and leftover chicken combine in this creamy casserole
that is topped off with French-fried onions.*

2¾ cups frozen pre-cooked
    shredded hash browns
    (8 ounces)

  1 16-ounce package frozen
    vegetable combination
    (broccoli, carrots, and
    water chestnuts)

1½ cups cubed cooked chicken

  1 10¾-ounce can condensed
    cream of mushroom soup

 ½ cup water

 ⅓ cup reduced-calorie sour
    cream

5–6 drops hot pepper sauce

 ½ cup French-fried onions

1. Combine frozen hash browns and vegetables in 2-quart microwave-safe casserole. Cover with casserole lid.

2. MICROWAVE (high) 11–13 minutes or until tender, stirring once. Stir in chicken, soup, water, sour cream, and pepper sauce. Cover.

3. MICROWAVE (high) 4–5 minutes or until heated through, stirring once. Sprinkle with onions.

4. MICROWAVE (high), uncovered, 1–1½ minutes or until onions are heated.

TIPS

● Cream of chicken or cream of celery soup can be substituted for mushroom.

● If watching salt intake, use low-sodium soup.

● An 8-ounce package of frozen hash brown patties can be substituted for loose hash browns. Increase time in step 2 to 12–14 minutes, stirring twice.

QUICK LINGUINE DELITE

**About 4 servings,
275 calories each**

It takes just five ingredients to come up with this tasty Italian dish. Keep extra cooked chicken in the freezer so you can enjoy it often.

4 ounces uncooked linguine

3 cups cubed zucchini (about 3 medium)

1½ cups cubed cooked chicken (about 6 ounces)

1 15½-ounce jar spaghetti sauce

2 tablespoons grated Parmesan cheese

1. Cook linguine as directed on package. Drain, rinse, and set aside.

2. Place zucchini in 4-cup microwave-safe measure. Cover with plastic wrap.

3. MICROWAVE (high) 4–5 minutes or until tender. Arrange linguine in 8-inch round microwave-safe baking dish. Top with zucchini, chicken, and spaghetti sauce. Sprinkle with Parmesan cheese. Cover with plastic wrap.

4. MICROWAVE (high) 4–5 minutes or until heated through and zucchini is tender.

TIPS

● Cubed cooked turkey can be substituted for chicken.

● When fresh zucchini is not available, substitute a 10-ounce package frozen chopped broccoli. Microwave (high) in package 3–4 minutes before adding to linguine.

● If substituting homemade spaghetti sauce, use 2 cups.

● Other favorite pastas can be substituted for linguine.

TEX-MEX CHICKEN TACOS

**8 tacos,
160 calories each**

Spinach and chicken make up the nutritious filling in these change-of-pace tacos.

¼ cup chopped green pepper

1½ cups cubed cooked chicken

1 cup taco sauce

8 taco shells

2 cups chopped fresh spinach

1 small tomato, chopped

½ cup shredded cheddar cheese

¼ cup chopped ripe olives

1. Place green pepper in 1-quart microwave-safe casserole. Cover with casserole lid.

2. MICROWAVE (high) 1–1½ minutes or until tender-crisp. Stir in chicken and taco sauce. Cover.

3. MICROWAVE (high) 3–3½ minutes or until heated through. To serve, spoon about ¼ cup chicken mixture into each taco shell. Top each with ¼ cup spinach, about 1 tablespoon each tomato and cheese, and ½ tablespoon olives.

TIPS

● When starting with raw chicken, cube 6 ounces. Add to green pepper and increase time in step 2 to 3–4 minutes or until chicken is done, stirring once.

● Lettuce can be substituted for spinach.

TURKEY AND FETTUCCINI ALFREDO

**About 4 servings,
350 calories each**

Turkey cutlets are combined with frozen fettuccini and vegetables for a delicious gourmet meal that's table-ready in just minutes.

1 10-ounce package frozen prepared fettuccini noodles Alfredo

2 cups frozen vegetable combination (broccoli, cauliflower, and carrots)

1 tablespoon dry bread crumbs

1 tablespoon grated Parmesan cheese

½ teaspoon paprika

⅛ teaspoon garlic salt

8 ounces turkey breast cutlets, cut into 4 pieces

1. Make small slit in pouch of noodles to allow steam to escape. Place pouch in microwave oven.

2. MICROWAVE (high) 3–4 minutes or until thawed. Place vegetables in 8-inch square microwave-safe baking dish. Stir in noodles. Cover with plastic wrap.

3. MICROWAVE (high) 5–6 minutes or until heated through, stirring once. Combine bread crumbs, cheese, paprika, and garlic salt on waxed paper; mix well. Coat both sides of cutlets with mixture; arrange on noodle mixture. Cover with plastic wrap.

4. MICROWAVE (high) 3½–4½ minutes or until cutlets are done.

TURKEY-TATER PIE

**About 5 servings,
310 calories each**

Mashed potatoes top a blend of turkey and vegetables for a quick and easy main dish.

1 pound ground turkey

*1 tablespoon instant minced
onion*

*1 16-ounce package frozen
Japanese-style vegetables*

*1 10¾-ounce can condensed
tomato soup*

*2 cups mashed potatoes
(without margarine)*

¼ cup shredded cheddar cheese

1. Crumble turkey into 2-quart microwave-safe casserole; add onion.

2. MICROWAVE (high), uncovered, 5–6 minutes or until turkey is no longer pink, stirring once. Stir in vegetables and soup. Cover with casserole lid.

3. MICROWAVE (high) 8–10 minutes or until vegetables are tender, stirring once. Spoon mounds of potato onto vegetable mixture. Cover with casserole lid.

4. MICROWAVE (high) 2–3 minutes or until potatoes are hot. Sprinkle with cheese. Let stand covered a few minutes to melt cheese.

TIPS

● Extra-lean ground beef can be substituted for turkey.

● When you do not have mashed potatoes on hand, prepare using instant variety.

MEXICAN TURKEY TORTILLAS

**About 4 servings,
320 calories each**

Taco-flavored ground turkey and corn are served inside tortillas in this quick meal. A fruit salad would complement the flavors nicely.

½ *pound ground turkey*

1 *10-ounce package frozen Mexican-style corn*

4 *flour tortillas (about 7-inch size)*

2 *tablespoons taco sauce*

¼ *cup shredded cheddar cheese*

¼ *cup sliced ripe olives*

1. Crumble turkey into 1-quart microwave-safe casserole; add frozen corn. Cover with casserole lid.

2. MICROWAVE (high) 8–10 minutes or until turkey is no longer pink, stirring once. Divide mixture among the four flour tortillas, using about ½ cup each. Roll up with filling inside. Place seam side down in 8-inch square microwave-safe baking dish. Cover with waxed paper.

3. MICROWAVE (high) 2–3 minutes or until heated through. Top with taco sauce; sprinkle with cheese and olives.

TIPS

- Picante sauce can be substituted for taco sauce.

- Corn tortillas can also be used.

- Extra-lean ground beef can be substituted for turkey.

QUICK CHOW MEIN

**About 5 servings,
250 calories each**

This recipe is quicker than stopping at your favorite Chinese restaurant for "take-out".

½ *pound ground turkey*

1 cup sliced celery

½ *cup chopped green pepper*

*1 10¾-ounce can condensed
cream of celery soup*

1 cup quick-cooking rice

1 cup water

1 tablespoon soy sauce

Dash pepper

1 cup chow mein noodles

1. Combine turkey, celery, and green pepper in 1½-quart microwave-safe casserole. Cover with casserole lid.

2. MICROWAVE (high) 4–5 minutes or until turkey is no longer pink and vegetables are tender, stirring once. Add soup, rice, water, soy sauce, and pepper. Cover.

3. MICROWAVE (high) 7–9 minutes or until rice is tender, stirring once. Sprinkle with chow mein noodles just before serving.

TIPS

● Cubed cooked chicken or turkey can be substituted for ground turkey. Add about 2 cups in step 1; reduce time in step 2 to 3–4 minutes.

● Individual servings can be frozen, but freeze chow mein noodles separately. To reheat, microwave (high) 4–5 minutes, stirring once. Sprinkle with chow mein noodles.

DIVINE FISH AND VEGETABLES

About 4 servings, 250 calories each

Cheesy vegetables top this easy fish and rice dish.

1 10-ounce package frozen broccoli, cauliflower, and carrots in cheese sauce

1 tablespoon margarine

½ cup shredded carrot (1 medium)

1 cup quick-cooking rice

1 cup hot water

12 ounces orange roughy fillets

2 tablespoons dry bread crumbs

1 teaspoon parsley flakes

½ teaspoon paprika

¼ teaspoon seasoned salt

1. Make small slit in pouch of vegetables to allow steam to escape. Place pouch in microwave oven.

2. MICROWAVE (high) 6–7 minutes or until heated. Set aside. Combine margarine and carrot in 10- by 6-inch microwave-safe baking dish. Cover with plastic wrap.

3. MICROWAVE (high) 3–4 minutes or until hot. Stir in rice and water. Arrange fillets on rice mixture. Combine crumbs, parsley, paprika, and seasoned salt; mix well. Spoon onto fish. Cover with plastic wrap.

4. MICROWAVE (high) 8–10 minutes or until rice is tender and fish flakes apart easily with fork, rearranging dish once. Spoon vegetables from pouch onto fillets.

5. MICROWAVE (high), uncovered, 1–2 minutes or until heated through.

SHRIMP AND CRAB ROLL-UPS

About 4 servings, 220 calories each

Frozen broccoli in cheese sauce is the tasty base for these quick seafood tortillas.

1 10-ounce package frozen broccoli in cheese sauce

1 6-ounce package frozen shrimp and crabmeat

½ teaspoon basil leaves

4 flour tortillas (about 7-inch size)

1 small tomato, chopped

¼ cup sliced ripe olives

1. Make small slit in pouch of broccoli to allow steam to escape. Place in microwave oven.

2. MICROWAVE (high) 5–6 minutes or until hot. Combine with shrimp and basil in small dish. Stir until shrimp and crabmeat are thawed. Divide mixture among flour tortillas, using about ½ cup each. Roll up with filling inside. Place seam side down in 10- by 6-inch microwave-safe baking dish. Cover with waxed paper.

3. MICROWAVE (high) 3–4 minutes or until heated through. Garnish with tomato and olives.

TIPS

• Cut-up imitation crabmeat sticks can be substituted for shrimp and crab.

• Cubed cooked chicken is also good. Use about 1½ cups.

SEAFOOD CASSEROLE

**About 4 servings,
180 calories each**

*Frozen macaroni and cheese becomes special when teamed with vegetables and crabmeat.
Elegant, yet easy.*

2 8-ounce packages frozen
   macaroni and cheese

1 10-ounce package frozen
   chopped broccoli

1 6-ounce package frozen
   crabmeat

1 teaspoon Worcestershire sauce

¼ teaspoon dill weed

1. Make small slit in each pouch of macaroni to allow steam to escape. Place pouches in microwave oven side by side with broccoli (remove foil overwrap if necessary).

2. MICROWAVE (high) 8–10 minutes or until each is hot, rearranging once if necessary. Drain broccoli. Combine macaroni and cheese, broccoli, crabmeat, Worcestershire sauce, and dill weed in 1-quart microwave-safe casserole. Cover with casserole lid.

3. MICROWAVE (high) 4–5 minutes or until heated through, stirring twice.

TIPS

- If crabmeat is thawed, reduce time in step 3 to 2–3 minutes.

- Cut-up imitation crabmeat sticks can be substituted for crabmeat.

- Drained water-packed tuna can be substituted for crabmeat.

TUNA-ON-A-MUFFIN

**About 6 servings,
140 calories each**

Vegetables in a lite cream sauce crown tuna-topped English muffins.

*3 English muffins, split and
   toasted*

*1 cup finely chopped fresh or
   frozen broccoli*

½ cup sliced fresh mushrooms

1 tablespoon chopped onion

1 tablespoon margarine

½ cup skim milk

1 tablespoon flour

⅛ teaspoon salt

*1 medium tomato, cut into
   6 slices*

*1 6½-ounce can water-packed
   tuna, drained*

1. Arrange muffins split side up on microwave-safe serving plate; set aside.

2. Combine broccoli, mushrooms, onion, and margarine in 2-cup microwave-safe measure.

3. MICROWAVE (high), uncovered, 4–5 minutes or until vegetables are tender. Add milk; mix in flour and salt until blended.

4. MICROWAVE (high), uncovered, 2–3 minutes or until mixture boils and thickens, stirring once. Top each muffin with a tomato slice; divide tuna among muffins; spread evenly. Spoon scant ¼ cup vegetable mixture onto each muffin half.

5. MICROWAVE (high), uncovered, 1–1½ minutes or until heated, rotating plate once.

TIP

● Canned crabmeat can be substituted for tuna.

BEEF AND VEGETABLE STROGANOFF

**About 5 servings,
310 calories each**

*Although this recipe has a few more ingredients than most in this chapter, you will find
the preparation to be quick and easy.*

*2 cups uncooked noodles
(4 ounces)*

*2 cups frozen vegetable
combination (broccoli,
cauliflower, and carrots)*

1 pound sirloin steak, sliced thin

*1 teaspoon natural meat
browning and seasoning
powder*

1 small onion, sliced

1 clove garlic, minced

*1 cup (4 ounces) sliced fresh
mushrooms*

1 teaspoon instant beef bouillon

¼ cup water

1 tablespoon flour

*1 tablespoon dry red wine or
water*

*¾ cup reduced-calorie sour
cream*

1. Cook noodles as directed on package. Drain, rinse, and set aside.

2. Place vegetables in 1½-quart microwave-safe casserole. Cover with casserole lid.

3. MICROWAVE (high) 5–6 minutes or until tender-crisp. Sprinkle meat with browning powder; toss to coat evenly. Add meat to vegetables along with onion, garlic, mushrooms, bouillon, and water; mix lightly. Cover.

4. MICROWAVE (high) 6–6½ minutes or until meat is no longer pink, stirring once. Combine flour and wine until smooth; stir into meat mixture.

5. MICROWAVE (high), uncovered, 3–4 minutes or until mixture boils and thickens, stirring once. Stir in sour cream. Arrange noodles on microwave-safe serving platter. Top with beef mixture.

6. MICROWAVE (high), uncovered, 2–3 minutes or until heated through.

TIPS

- If browning powder is not available, brown meat in ½ tablespoon oil over medium-high heat on range.

- Individual servings can be frozen. To reheat, add 1 tablespoon water and microwave (high) 4–5 minutes, rotating dish once.

CHINESE BEEF WITH VEGETABLES

About 4 servings, 205 calories each

Frozen vegetables and quick-cooking rice make this dish easy to prepare. Partially freeze meat to assure paper-thin slices.

1 cup water

1 cup quick-cooking rice

2 cups frozen vegetable combination (broccoli, green beans, and mushrooms)

1 clove garlic, minced

½ pound boneless sirloin steak, sliced thin

½ teaspoon natural meat browning and seasoning powder

¼ cup water

1 tablespoon cornstarch

3 tablespoons soy sauce

1. MICROWAVE (high) 1 cup water in uncovered 2-cup microwave-safe measure 2–3 minutes or until boiling. Stir in rice. Let stand.

2. Combine vegetables and garlic in 1½-quart microwave-safe casserole. Cover with casserole lid.

3. MICROWAVE (high) 2–2½ minutes or until vegetables are tender-crisp. Sprinkle meat with browning powder; add to vegetables along with water, cornstarch, and soy sauce. Mix well; cover.

4. MICROWAVE (high) 7–8 minutes or until meat is no longer pink and sauce is thickened, stirring twice. Spoon rice onto microwave-safe serving plate. Top with meat mixture.

5. MICROWAVE (high), uncovered, 2–3 minutes or until heated through.

TIPS

- Other favorite vegetable combinations can be substituted.

- If browning powder is not available, sprinkle meat with unseasoned meat tenderizer and add ½ teaspoon instant beef bouillon with soy sauce.

- Individual servings can be frozen. To reheat, microwave (high) 4–5 minutes, rotating dish once.

CHEESEBURGER-VEGETABLE PIE

**About 6 servings,
230 calories each**

This easy-to-serve main dish pie is perfect for lunch, brunch, or supper.

½ *pound lean ground beef*

1 *small onion, chopped*

1 *10-ounce package frozen broccoli, cauliflower, and carrots in cheese sauce*

¾ *cup buttermilk baking mix*

1¼ *cups skim milk*

2 *eggs*

½ *teaspoon dry mustard*

5–6 *drops hot pepper sauce*

¼ *cup shredded cheddar cheese*

1 *small tomato, chopped*

1. Crumble ground beef into 9-inch microwave-safe pie plate; add onion. Make a small slit in pouch of vegetables to allow steam to escape. Place pie plate and vegetables side by side in microwave oven.

2. MICROWAVE (high), uncovered, 9–10 minutes or until meat is no longer pink. Stir to break meat into small pieces; drain. Add vegetables; mix well.

3. Combine baking mix, milk, eggs, mustard, and pepper sauce in blender or mixing bowl. Process 15 seconds in blender or beat with hand beater until smooth. Pour over meat mixture.

4. MICROWAVE (high), uncovered, 6–7 minutes or until edges are set, rotating plate once. Then, MICROWAVE (medium—50%), uncovered, 4–5 minutes or until center is just about set, rotating plate once. Sprinkle with cheese and tomato. Let stand about 10 minutes before cutting into wedges and serving.

TIP

• Full power is not recommended with this recipe.

CHILI STEW

**About 4 servings,
300 calories each**

This lite version of chili is made quickly using a seasoning mix.

½ *pound lean ground beef*

1 *small onion, chopped*

1 *cup chopped green pepper*

1 *16-ounce can tomatoes,
undrained*

1 *16-ounce can mixed
vegetables, undrained*

1 *15-ounce can kidney beans,
undrained*

1 *1¼-ounce envelope chili
seasoning mix*

1. Crumble ground beef into 2-quart microwave-safe casserole. Add onion and green pepper.
2. MICROWAVE (high), uncovered, 4–5 minutes or until meat is no longer pink, stirring once. Drain. Add tomatoes (cut tomatoes into small pieces), vegetables, beans, and seasoning mix; stir lightly. Cover with casserole lid.
3. MICROWAVE (high) 10–12 minutes or until mixture boils and flavors are blended, stirring once.

TIP

● Individual servings can be frozen. To reheat, microwave (high) 7–8 minutes, stirring once.

HOME-STYLE CASSEROLE

**About 6 servings,
260 calories each**

Frozen vegetables extend this macaroni casserole into an easy one-dish meal.

½ *pound lean ground beef*

1 *small onion, chopped*

1 *15½-ounce jar spaghetti
sauce*

1 *cup uncooked macaroni
(4 ounces)*

1¼ *cups hot water*

½ *teaspoon garlic salt*

2 *cups frozen vegetable
combination (broccoli,
cauliflower, and carrots)*

1 *cup (4 ounces) shredded
mozzarella cheese*

1. Crumble ground beef into 2-quart microwave-safe casserole. Add onion.
2. MICROWAVE (high), uncovered, 2½–3½ minutes or until no longer pink, stirring once. Drain. Add spaghetti sauce, macaroni, water, and garlic salt; mix lightly. Cover with casserole lid.
3. MICROWAVE (high) 7–8 minutes or until just about boiling, stirring once. Mix in vegetables; cover.
4. MICROWAVE (high) 10–12 minutes or until macaroni and vegetables are tender, stirring twice. Stir in cheese. Let stand a few minutes to melt cheese.

TIP

● Individual servings can be frozen. To reheat, add 1 tablespoon water and microwave (high) 4–5 minutes, stirring once.

ONE-DISH CHOP SUEY

This easy Oriental dish combines ground beef, rice, Chinese cabbage, and tomatoes.

½ **pound lean ground beef**

2 **green onions, cut into ½-inch
pieces (including tops)**

⅓ **cup chopped green pepper**

⅛ **teaspoon garlic powder**

1 **cup quick-cooking rice**

4 **cups sliced Chinese cabbage
(Napa)**

1 **16-ounce can beef broth**

1 **tablespoon cornstarch**

1 **tablespoon soy sauce**

1 **tablespoon dry sherry
(optional)**

1 **tomato, cut into wedges**

1. Crumble ground beef into 1½-quart microwave-safe casserole. Add onions and green pepper.

2. MICROWAVE (high), uncovered, 2½–3½ minutes or until no longer pink, stirring once. Drain. Stir in garlic powder, rice, cabbage, and beef broth. Combine cornstarch, soy sauce, and sherry; mix until smooth. Stir into cabbage mixture. Cover with casserole lid.

3. MICROWAVE (high) 10–12 minutes or until mixture boils and thickens, stirring twice. Add tomato; mix lightly.

4. MICROWAVE (high), uncovered, 1–2 minutes or until tomato is heated.

ITALIAN SPAGHETTI WITH PORK

About 5 servings, 325 calories each

Pork, being naturally tender, cooks quickly in this lite version of a popular favorite.

4 ounces uncooked spaghetti

1 tablespoon cooking oil

1 pound cubed boneless pork

2 tablespoons chopped onion

½ cup sliced fresh mushrooms

½ cup sliced celery

½ cup sliced carrot (about 1 medium)

1 15½-ounce jar spaghetti sauce

1. Cook spaghetti as directed on package. Rinse, drain, and set aside.

2. Heat oil in shallow 1½-quart pyroceramic casserole over medium-high heat on range. Add pork and brown on all sides. Add onion, mushrooms, celery, and carrot. Cover with casserole lid.

3. MICROWAVE (high) 5–6 minutes or until vegetables are tender-crisp, stirring once. Stir in spaghetti sauce. Cover.

4. MICROWAVE (high) 7–8 minutes or until meat is tender, stirring once. Arrange spaghetti on microwave-safe serving plate. Top with sauce.

5. MICROWAVE (high), uncovered, 2–3 minutes or until heated through.

TIPS

- A little Parmesan cheese can be sprinkled on meat mixture before heating in step 5. Each tablespoon adds about seven calories/serving.

- If substituting your own favorite spaghetti sauce, use about 2 cups.

- Cubed cooked pork can be used. Omit oil and browning in step 2; add 3 cups pork with vegetables.

- Individual servings can be frozen. To reheat, add 2 tablespoons water and microwave (high) 5–6 minutes, rotating dish twice.

PORK AND NOODLES

**About 4 servings,
235 calories each**

Frozen vegetables, cooked pork, and Oriental noodles are combined in this easy one-dish meal.

2 **cups frozen vegetable combination (broccoli, cauliflower, and carrots)**

2 **cups cubed cooked pork**

1 **3-ounce package Oriental-flavor ramen noodle soup mix**

1 **16-ounce can tomatoes, undrained**

½ **cup water**

1. Place vegetables in 1½-quart microwave-safe casserole. Cover with casserole lid.

2. MICROWAVE (high) 3–4 minutes or until tender-crisp. Mix in pork, noodles (including seasoning packet), tomatoes (cut into small pieces), and water. Cover.

3. MICROWAVE (high) 6–7 minutes or until noodles are tender, stirring once or twice.

TIPS

● Chicken can be substituted for pork.

● When using fresh meat, cut 8 ounces into pieces. Add with frozen vegetables and stir mixture once during cooking.

HAM-VEGETABLE SOUP

About 4 servings, 240 calories each

This lite but filling soup is perfect for a chilly day. Complete the meal with crackers or crusty rolls and fresh fruit.

1 clove garlic, minced

2 tablespoons margarine

¼ cup unsifted all-purpose flour

1 teaspoon dry mustard

1 teaspoon instant chicken bouillon

½ teaspoon basil leaves

Dash pepper

4 cups skim milk

1 cup finely chopped cooked ham (about 4 ounces)

3 cups frozen vegetable combination (broccoli, cauliflower, and carrots)

1. Combine garlic and margarine in 2-quart microwave-safe casserole.

2. MICROWAVE (high), uncovered, 1–1½ minutes or until garlic is tender. Stir in flour, mustard, bouillon, basil, and pepper. Slowly blend in milk, stirring until smooth. Add ham and vegetables.

3. MICROWAVE (high), uncovered, 18–20 minutes or until mixture boils and thickens, stirring every 5 minutes.

TIP

● Cooked chicken, turkey, or turkey-ham can be substituted for ham.

HAM-POTATO FRITTATA

**About 4 servings,
130 calories each**

This combination of ham, potatoes, and eggs makes a nutritious lunch, brunch, or supper.

2 green onions, sliced (including tops)

2 tablespoons chopped green pepper

1 tablespoon margarine

2 cups frozen pre-cooked shredded hash browns (6 ounces)

4 eggs

2 tablespoons water

¼ teaspoon salt

1 cup cubed cooked ham (about 4 ounces)

2 tablespoons grated Parmesan cheese

1. Combine onions, green pepper, and margarine in 9-inch microwave-safe pie plate.

2. MICROWAVE (high), uncovered, 1½–2 minutes or until tender-crisp. Add hash browns; mix lightly. Cover with plastic wrap.

3. MICROWAVE (high) 5–6 minutes or until heated through, stirring once. Beat together eggs, water, and salt; pour over potatoes. Sprinkle with ham. Cover with plastic wrap.

4. MICROWAVE (high) 4–5 minutes or until edges are set. Gently move cooked portion to center. Sprinkle with cheese. Cover.

5. MICROWAVE (high) 1–2 minutes or until center is just about set. Let stand covered about 5 minutes before serving.

TIPS

• Turkey-ham can be substituted for regular ham.

• If watching cholesterol, use 1 cup thawed frozen egg substitute for the eggs.

TORTELLINI-VEGETABLE SUPPER

About 5 servings, 200 calories each

A lite cream sauce with just a hint of wine combines with tortellini, frozen vegetables, and ham for a special, but easy dinner.

1 7-ounce package cheese-filled tortellini

3 cups frozen vegetable combination (broccoli, cauliflower, and carrots)

2 tablespoons margarine

2 tablespoons flour

1½ cups skim milk

1 teaspoon instant chicken bouillon

1 cup cubed cooked ham (about 4 ounces)

1 tablespoon dry white wine (optional)

¼ cup grated Parmesan cheese

1. Cook tortellini as directed on package. Drain and set aside.

2. Combine vegetables and margarine in 2-quart microwave-safe casserole. Cover with casserole lid.

3. MICROWAVE (high) 6–7 minutes or until tender-crisp. Blend in flour. Stir in milk, bouillon, and ham.

4. MICROWAVE (high), uncovered, 6–7 minutes or until mixture boils and thickens slightly, stirring twice. Stir in tortellini and wine. Sprinkle with cheese.

5. MICROWAVE (high), uncovered, 2–3 minutes or until heated through.

TIPS

- Other vegetable combinations can be substituted. Or, use a combination of fresh vegetables.

- Cooked chicken or pork can be substituted for ham.

CHEESY RICE COMBO

About 4 servings, 335 calories each

Seasoned rice mix is the base and Canadian bacon, pea pods, and cheese spread add the flavorful extras that make this recipe special.

1 4.7-ounce envelope rice and sauce with vegetables almondine

2 cups hot water

1 6-ounce package Canadian bacon, cubed (about 1½ cups)

1 6-ounce package frozen pea pods

½ cup pasteurized process cheese spread (Cheez Whiz)

1. Combine rice mix and water in 2-quart microwave-safe casserole.

2. MICROWAVE (high), uncovered, 11–13 minutes or until rice is tender. Stir in Canadian bacon, pea pods, and cheese spread. Cover with casserole lid.

3. MICROWAVE (high) 3–4 minutes or until heated through, stirring once.

CARAWAY CABBAGE AND SAUSAGE

About 4 servings, 250 calories each

This lite, but hearty dish has a German flair. Serve it with rye bread or rolls.

3 cups shredded cabbage

2 medium potatoes, peeled and cubed (about 2 cups)

1 medium apple, cored and chopped

2 tablespoons water

½ teaspoon salt

¼ teaspoon ground allspice

¼–½ teaspoon caraway seed

1 10-ounce package fully cooked low-fat smoked sausage links

1. Combine cabbage, potatoes, apple, water, salt, allspice, and caraway in 1-quart microwave-safe casserole; mix lightly. Cover with casserole lid.

2. MICROWAVE (high) 10–12 minutes or until cabbage and potatoes are tender, stirring once. Cut sausages into ½-inch pieces. Add to cabbage; mix lightly. Cover.

3. MICROWAVE (high) 2–3 minutes or until heated through.

POCKET PIZZAS

About 6 servings, 180 calories each

Pita breads make handy take-along sandwiches when filled with a tasty pizzalike mixture.

1 10-ounce package frozen chopped broccoli (about 2 cups)

½ cup sliced fresh mushrooms

1 8-ounce can pizza sauce

3 ounces sliced pepperoni

3 pita breads (6-inch size)

¾ cup (3 ounces) shredded mozzarella cheese

¼ cup sliced ripe olives

1. Combine broccoli and mushrooms in 1-quart microwave-safe casserole. Cover with casserole lid.

2. MICROWAVE (high) 4–5 minutes or until tender-crisp, stirring once. Mix in pizza sauce. Cut pepperoni slices in half; stir into vegetable mixture.

3. Cut each pita bread in half vertically; open each half to form a pocket. Spoon about ½ cup vegetable mixture into each and place on microwave-safe serving plate. Sprinkle each with 2 tablespoons cheese. Top with olives.

4. MICROWAVE (high), uncovered, 1½–2 minutes or until cheese is melted, rotating plate once.

TIP

● Sliced fresh zucchini can be substituted for broccoli.

MANICOTTI-IN-A-TORTILLA

**About 6 servings,
275 calories each**

Flour tortillas make the simple wrappers for this manicotti filling that features frozen spinach soufflé.

1 *12-ounce package frozen spinach soufflé*

2 *cups shredded carrot (about 4 medium)*

1 *cup ricotta cheese*

5–6 *drops hot pepper sauce*

6 *flour tortillas (about 10-inch size)*

1 *8-ounce can tomato sauce*

½ *cup water*

½ *teaspoon oregano leaves*

1. Transfer soufflé from package to 1-quart microwave-safe casserole. Add carrots. Cover with casserole lid.

2. MICROWAVE (medium—50%) 7–8 minutes or until soufflé is thawed and carrots are tender, stirring once. Stir cheese and hot pepper sauce into mixture. Divide mixture among tortillas. Roll up with filling inside. Place seam side down in 12- by 8-inch microwave-safe baking dish. Combine tomato sauce, water, and oregano. Spoon over tortillas. Cover with plastic wrap.

3. MICROWAVE (medium—50%) 15–17 minutes or until filling is set, rotating dish once.

TIPS

● To use full power instead of medium power in step 2, microwave 3–4 minutes, stirring every minute. In step 3, use intervals of 3 minutes microwave and 3 minutes stand for the 15–17 minutes.

● If using smaller tortillas, increase the number used.

VEGETABLE LASAGNA ROLLS

About 6 servings, 215 calories each

Lasagna takes a new shape when it is rolled around a creamy cheese mixture. A vegetarian spaghetti sauce tops these easy rolls.

6 uncooked lasagna noodles

2 cups frozen vegetable combination (broccoli, cauliflower, and carrots)

2 tablespoons water

1 15½-ounce jar spaghetti sauce

1 cup low-fat cottage cheese

¾ cup (3 ounces) shredded mozzarella cheese

1 tablespoon snipped fresh parsley

1 egg

1. Cook lasagna noodles as directed on package. Rinse, drain, and set aside.

2. Combine vegetables and water in 1-quart microwave-safe casserole. Cover with casserole lid.

3. MICROWAVE (high) 4–5 minutes or until tender-crisp. Mix in spaghetti sauce; set aside. Combine cottage cheese, ½ cup of the mozzarella cheese, parsley, and egg; mix well. Lay noodles out flat; divide cheese mixture evenly among noodles. Roll up with cheese mixture inside. Place seam side down in 8-inch round microwave-safe baking dish. Top with vegetable mixture. Cover with waxed paper.

4. MICROWAVE (high) 7–8 minutes or until heated through, rotating dish once. Sprinkle with remaining ¼ cup cheese. Let stand a few minutes to melt cheese.

TIPS

● Other favorite vegetable combinations can be substituted.

● If substituting homemade spaghetti sauce, use 2 cups.

CHAPTER

8
CONVENIENCE FOODS FOR EASY ONE-DISH MEALS

Today there are many convenience foods on the grocery shelves and in the freezer cases that lend themselves well to microwave cooking. A few are designated as "lite," but many more can be transformed into lite one-dish meals with the addition of a few simple ingredients.

In this chapter, we have taken a variety of convenience foods and shown how to extend and lighten them so they qualify for "lite," one-dish eating. Fresh or frozen vegetables have been added depending on which seemed to be most appropriate for the particular convenience product. By making combinations, we not only improve the overall nutritional value, but also cut the sometimes high salt level as well as the high price of individual entrees.

Often there is more than one brand available for some of the convenience foods used. We have given the package weight in the recipes. Try to select a package that is close in weight so the additions and timings will work.

When there is more than one brand, there are likely to be different microwave cooking methods suggested on the packages. We have selected the method that we feel is best and suggest using it even if the package has different microwave directions.

With many of the mixes, it is often necessary to add water to aid in the cooking and rehydration. To speed the process, we call for hot water. By this, we mean hot tap water. This method is usually much faster than waiting for the microwave to heat cold water.

When two different types of convenience foods are combined in a recipe, we sometimes direct you to combine the foods in one dish for heating and other times we recommend heating the containers side by side in the microwave oven. Microwaves are attracted to foods differently. If you find that one container or package is heated before another, remove it and give the other a few more seconds or minutes, as needed.

Pouches of frozen food need to have a small slit made in the plastic to allow excess steam to escape. Otherwise, the steam from the hot food may cause the pouch to swell and burst during the heating process. A small slit is all that is necessary. When manipulating the package as an aid to defrosting and heating, be careful that the food does not come through the opening.

There are many things you can do with convenience foods to make them your own special creations. Use the examples in this chapter as starters. The basic directions will be the same as you try other flavors and combinations of similar convenience products. You will be surprised at how many appetizing creations you can come up with using your favorite mixes or frozen convenience foods.

CHICKEN 'N' RICE COMBO

**About 4 servings,
260 calories each**

Add Oriental vegetables and chicken strips to packaged rice mix and you have a special meal, indeed.

1 4½-ounce package microwave chicken-flavored rice and vermicelli mix

1¾ cups hot water

1 tablespoon margarine

1 10-ounce package frozen stir-fry vegetables with seasoning packet

8 ounces skinned and boned chicken breast, cut into strips

1. Combine rice and vermicelli mix (including seasoning packet), water, margarine, vegetables (including seasoning packet), and chicken in 2-quart microwave-safe casserole. Cover with casserole lid.

2. MICROWAVE (high) 18–20 minutes or until rice has absorbed liquid and chicken is done, stirring twice. Let stand about 5 minutes before serving.

TIP

● These timings are for the microwave rice and vermicelli mix. When using regular rice, the cooking time will be slightly longer.

CHICKEN 'N' STUFFING WITH BRUSSELS SPROUTS

**About 4 servings,
340 calories each**

This recipe teams stuffing, cooked chicken, and brussels sprouts for a quick-to-fix meal.

1½ cups frozen diced cooked chicken

1¾ cups hot water

3 tablespoons margarine

1 6-ounce package chicken-flavored saucepan-type stuffing mix

1 10-ounce package frozen brussels sprouts

1. Combine chicken, water, margarine, and seasoning packet from stuffing mix in 2-quart microwave-safe casserole. Cover with casserole lid. Place side by side with package of brussels sprouts (remove foil overwrap if necessary) in microwave oven.

2. MICROWAVE (high) 8–10 minutes or until water mixture boils. Stir in stuffing crumbs packet; mix lightly. Arrange brussels sprouts around edge of dish. Cover.

3. MICROWAVE (high) 2–3 minutes or until vegetables are tender.

TIP

● Cooked cubed chicken can be substituted for frozen variety.

EASY CHICKEN CHOW MEIN

**About 4 servings,
270 calories each**

The vegetables and rice cook side-by-side in this Chinese-type dish.

1 22¼-ounce package chow
  mein dinner mix

2 cups hot water

½ teaspoon salt

1 6¾-ounce can chunk chicken

1 10-ounce package frozen
  Chinese-style vegetables with
  seasonings

1. Combine rice (in bag from mix), hot water, and salt in 1-quart microwave-safe casserole. Cover with casserole lid. Combine vegetables and sauce (from mix), chicken, and frozen vegetables (save seasoning packet for another use or this dish will be too salty) in 1-quart microwave-safe casserole. Cover with casserole lid. Place both dishes side by side in microwave oven.

2. MICROWAVE (high) 22–24 minutes or until rice is done and vegetables are tender, stirring vegetables once and turning bag of rice over once.

TIP

● Cubed cooked chicken can be substituted for canned. Use about 1½ cups.

POTATO A LA KING

**About 1 serving,
240 calories**

Turn frozen creamed chicken into a baked potato filling, fit for a king.

1 medium potato

½ cup frozen peas and carrots

1 4-ounce package frozen
  chicken à la king

1. Prick potato several times with fork. Place in microwave oven on paper towel.

2. MICROWAVE (high) 4–5 minutes or until just about tender, turning potato over once. Set aside. Combine peas and carrots and chicken à la king in 2-cup microwave-safe measure.

3. MICROWAVE (high), uncovered, 3–4 minutes or until heated through, stirring once. Make a lengthwise cut down center of potato, cutting almost through; press sides to open potato. Place on microwave-safe serving plate. Spoon chicken mixture into potato.

4. MICROWAVE (high), uncovered, 1–2 minutes or until heated through.

QUICK TURKEY DINNER FOR ONE

About 1 serving, 185 calories

A hash brown patty, frozen turkey in gravy, and a few fresh carrot coins combine for this easy-to-prepare meal.

½ *cup sliced carrot (1 small)*

3 *ounces frozen hash browns (1 patty)*

1 *5-ounce package frozen gravy and sliced turkey*

1. Place carrots on one side of microwave-safe serving plate. Place hash browns on other side of plate. Top hash browns with frozen turkey mixture. Cover with plastic wrap.
2. MICROWAVE (high) 5–6 minutes or until carrots and hash browns are tender, rotating plate once.

TIPS

● Other favorite fresh or frozen vegetables can be substituted for carrot.

● Other types of meat in gravy can be substituted.

LAYERED FISH DINNER

About 4 servings, 180 calories each

This combination, including three frozen foods, makes an appetizing layered dinner in just minutes.

1 *11-ounce package frozen French-style rice*

¼ *cup water*

1 *10-ounce package frozen broccoli in butter sauce*

1 *10-ounce package frozen individual sole fillets*

1. Place rice in 10- by 6-inch microwave-safe baking dish. Add water; sprinkle with seasoning packet from rice. Cover with plastic wrap. Make a small slit in pouch of vegetables. Place rice dish and vegetable pouch side by side in microwave oven.
2. MICROWAVE (high) 9–10 minutes or until both mixtures are hot, stirring rice once. Arrange frozen fillets on rice. Spoon vegetable mixture over fillets. Cover with plastic wrap.
3. MICROWAVE (high) 5–6 minutes or until fish flakes apart easily with fork.

TIPS

● Other favorite vegetables or combination vegetables in butter sauce can be substituted.

● If fish fillets are thawed, reduce time in step 3 to 3–4 minutes.

SHRIMP WITH NOODLES PARMESAN

**About 4 servings,
230 calories each**

Packaged mixes become gourmet delights when special ingredients like shrimp and pearl onions are added.

1½ cups hot water

½ cup skim milk

1 tablespoon margarine

1 4½-ounce envelope Parmesan noodles and sauce mix

1 10-ounce package frozen green peas and pearl onions

1 6-ounce package frozen cooked shrimp, rinsed

1. MICROWAVE (high) water in covered 1½-quart microwave-safe casserole 4–5 minutes or until boiling. Stir in milk, margarine, and noodle mix. Cover.

2. MICROWAVE (high) 4–5 minutes or until noodles are just about tender, stirring once. Add peas and shrimp. Cover.

3. MICROWAVE (high) 5–6 minutes or until heated through, stirring once. Let stand about 5 minutes before serving.

TIP

● Other cooked seafood or poultry can be substituted for shrimp. Use about 1½ cups.

SHRIMP CHOW MEIN CASSEROLE

**About 2 servings,
185 calories each**

Crunchy pea pods and quick-cooking rice are added to frozen shrimp chow mein. This dish is table-ready in just 15 minutes.

1 12-ounce package frozen shrimp chow mein

½ cup water

½ cup quick-cooking rice

1 6-ounce package frozen pea pods

Soy sauce (optional)

1. Combine chow mein and water in 1-quart microwave-safe casserole. Cover with casserole lid.

2. MICROWAVE (high) 8–10 minutes or until mixture is hot and bubbly, stirring twice. Stir in rice and pea pods. Cover.

3. MICROWAVE (high) 2–3 minutes or until hot. Let stand covered 5 minutes. Serve with soy sauce, if desired.

TIP

● A 10-ounce package frozen chopped broccoli or cut asparagus can be substituted for pea pods.

TUNA TETRAZZINI WITH VEGETABLES

**About 5 servings,
200 calories each**

A packaged spaghetti dinner mix is at its best with the additions of tuna and vegetables. It makes an easy supper the entire family will enjoy.

1 7-ounce package "add tuna" spaghetti and sauce dinner mix

2¾ cups hot water

¼ cup skim milk

1 tablespoon margarine

1 16-ounce package frozen vegetable combination (broccoli, cauliflower, and carrots)

1 6½-ounce can water-packed tuna, drained

1. Combine dinner mix (spaghetti, sauce, and cheese packets), water, milk, and margarine in 2-quart microwave-safe casserole. Stir in vegetables and tuna. Cover with casserole lid.

2. MICROWAVE (high) 24–26 minutes or until spaghetti and vegetables are tender, stirring twice. Let stand about 5 minutes before serving.

ITALIAN SPAGHETTI PLATTER

**About 1 serving,
310 calories**

Here's a fast way to turn a frozen entree into something extra special. French bread and a salad would complete the meal.

1 11½-ounce package frozen light-style spaghetti with mushroom sauce

1 small zucchini, sliced (⅔ cup)

½ tablespoon grated Parmesan cheese

1. Make small slit in spaghetti and sauce pouches to allow steam to escape. Place pouches side by side in microwave oven.

2. MICROWAVE (high) 4–5 minutes or until thawed, rearranging once. Place spaghetti on microwave-safe serving plate. Top with sauce. Arrange zucchini around edge of plate. Cover with plastic wrap.

3. MICROWAVE (high) 2–3 minutes or until zucchini is tender and entree is hot. Sprinkle with cheese.

CHIPPED BEEF ON TOAST

**About 2 servings,
350 calories each**

*Chipped beef has never been as appealing as when used to top broccoli spears and toast.
It makes a quick, nutritious lunch or supper for two.*

*1 11-ounce package frozen
creamed chipped beef*

*1 10-ounce package frozen
broccoli spears*

*2 slices thin-sliced wheat bread,
toasted*

1. Make small slit in chipped beef pouch. Place side-by-side with package of broccoli (remove foil outerwrap if necessary) in microwave oven.

2. MICROWAVE (high) 8–9 minutes or until sauce is heated and broccoli is tender, rearranging once.

3. Place a slice of toast on each of two microwave-safe serving plates. Top with broccoli, placing stems toward center. Spoon chipped beef over center, leaving some of broccoli flower portion showing.

4. MICROWAVE (high) both plates, uncovered, 1–1½ minutes or until hot.

TIP

● The broccoli and chipped beef are also good served on toasted English muffins.

SPANISH RICE AND PORK

**About 4 servings,
220 calories each**

*A seasoned rice and sauce mix combines with canned tomatoes and fresh pork for a
quick, tasty supper dish.*

*1 16-ounce can tomatoes,
undrained*

*1 16-ounce can zucchini,
undrained*

*1 4½-ounce envelope Spanish
rice and sauce mix*

½ pound cubed lean pork

*1 small green pepper, cut into
rings*

1. Combine tomatoes (cut tomatoes into small pieces), zucchini, rice mix, and pork in 1½-quart microwave-safe casserole. Cover with casserole lid.

2. MICROWAVE (high) 12–14 minutes or until liquid is absorbed, stirring once. Fluff with fork. Garnish with pepper rings. Let stand covered about 5 minutes before serving.

TIPS

● If using cubed cooked pork, add about 1½ cups.

● Fresh or cooked chicken can be substituted for pork.

HAM AND POTATOES AU GRATIN

**About 4 servings,
265 calories each**

Cooked ham, a packaged potato mix, and frozen green beans combine in this hearty main dish casserole.

1 5½-ounce package au gratin potato mix

2 cups hot water

2 tablespoons margarine

⅔ cup milk

2 cups cubed lean ham (about 8 ounces)

2 9-ounce packages frozen cut green beans

1. Combine dry potatoes (set aside seasoning packet), water, and margarine in 2-quart microwave-safe casserole. Cover with casserole lid.

2. MICROWAVE (high) 10–11 minutes or until potatoes are partially softened. Stir in milk, seasoning packet, and ham. Top with green beans. Cover.

3. MICROWAVE (high) 12–15 minutes or until potatoes and beans are tender, stirring once.

MACARONI AND CHEESE PLATE

**About 4 servings,
345 calories each**

Keep this recipe in mind when tomatoes are plentiful in the summer. Macaroni and cheese mix, with sausages added, tops juicy slices of fresh tomato.

3 cups hot water

1 7¼-ounce package macaroni and cheese dinner mix

¼ cup skim milk

1½ tablespoons margarine

½ 10-ounce package fully cooked low-fat smoked sausage links

2 medium tomatoes, sliced

Snipped fresh parsley

1. MICROWAVE (high) water in covered 2-quart microwave-safe casserole 8–9 minutes or until boiling. Stir in macaroni from dinner mix.

2. MICROWAVE (high), uncovered, 8–9 minutes or until macaroni is tender, stirring once. Drain. Stir in milk, margarine, and sauce mix. Cut sausages into ½-inch pieces; mix with macaroni. Arrange tomato slices on microwave-safe serving plate. Top with macaroni mixture.

3. MICROWAVE (high), uncovered, 3–4 minutes or until heated through. Garnish with parsley.

INDEX